The Eight Levels Of Homeowner Wealth Multiplication

Book #2 Of The

Homeowner Wealth Series

by Daniel R. Amerman, CFA

This book contain the ideas and opinions of the author. It is a conceptual exploration of financial and general economic principles. What this book does not contain is specific investment, legal, tax or any other form of professional advice. If specific advice is needed, it should be sought from an appropriate professional. Any liability, responsibility or warranty for the results of the application of principles contained in the book and related materials, either directly or indirectly, are expressly disclaimed by the author.

The cover graphic is from Chapter 5, and shows the sources of the increases in national average home equity from 1975 to 2019.

CONTENTS

Chapter 3
Multiplying Real Home Price Gains Times Inflation For Reliable Profits

Chapter 4
The History Of Eight Levels Of The Multiplication Of Wealth

Chapter 5
Mapping Out The 19 Sources Of Long Term Homeowner Gains

Chapter 6
Rapid Wealth Creation From Nineteen Sources
105

Chapter 7
Falling Real Home Prices & Using The Formula To Reduce Risk By 80%   119

Chapter 8
Getting Lucky & The 23% Chance Of Getting The Price Of A House For Free   141

Chapter 9
The National Debt & Future Wealth Maps   173

Chapter 10
Population Growth & Future Wealth Maps   205

Chapter One

Winning Lotteries & Profiting From The National Debt

How would you like to buy a ticket in a lottery where there was an almost one in four chance of winning the price of an entire home? What if the consolation prize - the average outcome for buying the ticket - was to quadruple your money in ten years?

Lots of people play the lottery, or gamble in casinos. In theory - each one of those gambles could indeed lead to a quarter million dollar or so gain.

In practice, however, very few people buy winning quarter million dollar lottery tickets, or walk out of a casino with an extra quarter million in their pocket. This is because the odds are extremely low of doing so, most people can play for their entire lives and not win such a large prize. Indeed, because the odds favor the "house", as in the state governments for lotteries, or the owners of the casinos - most people who try for the big wins will steadily lose money over the years instead.

Now, there is a "catch" when it comes to having a really good chance of winning the price of a home – which is that you have to first buy that home. That means you have to comfortably live your life in a nice home, perhaps with a garden in the back yard, and maybe in a good school district as well. And after ten years, what national average homeownership statistics show us is that there is a 23% chance that your home equity will have increased by an amount that is about equal to the entire original purchase price of the home.

That is an amazing and life changing outcome - which has happened in practice for many millions of homeowners over the decades. It isn't improbable or fantastic - but is instead just an average result, that has happened over and over again.

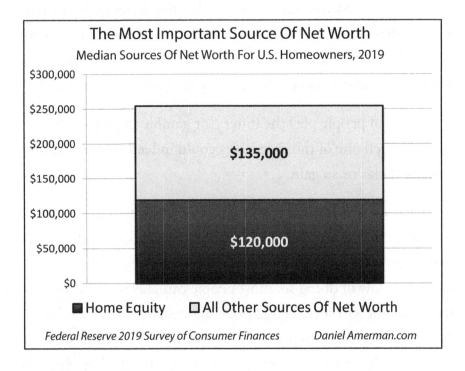

These extraordinary but average major increases in equity also explain why for the two thirds of the population who are homeowners, their home equity makes up about half of their median net worth, almost as much as all their savings, investments, retirement accounts and other assets combined (According to the Federal Reserve's 2019 *Survey Of Consumer Finances*).

In Book #1 in this series, "*The Homeowner Wealth Formula*", we examined in detail why homes have been such a good investment for so many millions of people over the decades. Using detailed historical information from almost four hundred different possible 1 to 10 year homeownership periods, we looked at the roles and importance of inflation, the compound interest formula, the multiplication and stacking that occurs when a home is bought with a mortgage, and how amortization increases both equity and safety.

Those first four levels of the multiplication of wealth together account for the great majority of the wealth creation from homeownership over the years, as well as the reliability of that wealth creation. In other words - the first four levels of homeowner wealth multiplication account for the great majority of about half of the net worth of about two thirds of U.S. households.

However, if one of the many millions of people who have become "house rich" from owning a home with a mortgage is asked about what the source was of half or more of their net worth - they aren't likely to talk about inflation, alignment with government policies, multiplying and stacking, or the compound interest formula.

Instead they are more likely to say something like *"I bought when home prices were much lower, the housing market went way up and I made a lot of money."*

On the face of it - that is a very accurate answer for most people. That is indeed what happened for so many millions of home buyers, again and again over the decades. But given that we are talking about the source of what is on average half of the net worth for two thirds of the population, it is likely worth digging a little deeper than that.

How accurate is that belief? How much of the very large national average increases in home equity have really come from the housing market going up, separate and aside from inflation or owning a home with a mortgage?

The Importance Of Market Changes For Home Equity

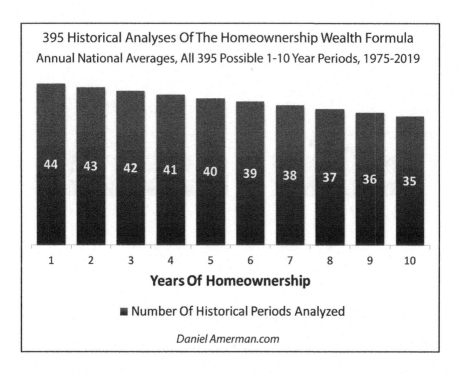

To find an accurate answer based on what history has to show us, we will begin by looking at 35 possible ten year home ownership periods between 1975 and 2019, starting with 1975 to 1985, and ending with 2009 to 2019.

When we look at national average home price changes for each of those ten year periods, using the Freddie Mac House Price Index, and also the individual mortgage amortizations using for national average mortgage rates in each starting year, as reported by the Federal Home Loan Mortgage Corporation (Freddie Mac), then we get 35 different increases in home equity, one for each ten year period.

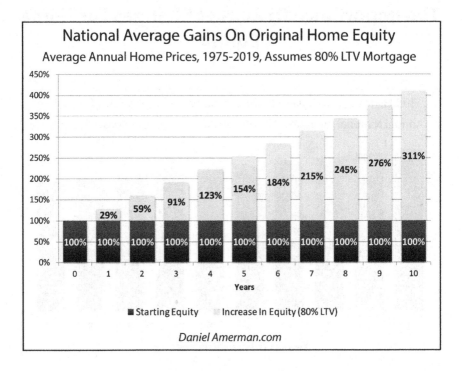

National Average Gains On Original Home Equity
Average Annual Home Prices, 1975-2019, Assumes 80% LTV Mortgage

Daniel Amerman.com

When we average the 35 ten year national average increases in home equity together, then we get the rightmost bar in the graph above. The national average outcome for homeowners in all their millions and across the decades, was to see a 311% gain in home equity, bringing total home equity to more than four times where it started.

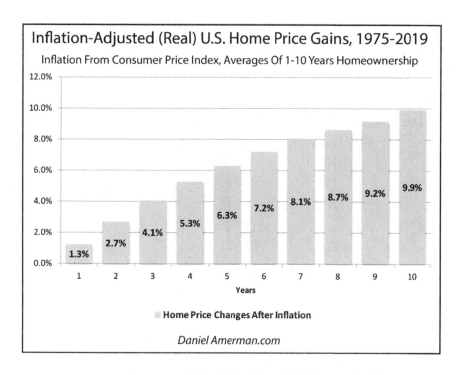

When we take that same Freddie Mac House Price Index for national average home prices in each year, and remove inflation using the Consumer Price Index (CPI-U) as reported by the U.S. Bureau of Labor Statistics, then we get the graph above. (There is much more about how this critical step is accomplished and the importance for homeowners and investors in the next chapter.)

The bottom line result is that when the inflation-adjusted home price changes for the nation are averaged together for 35 different ten year homeownership periods - the average homeowner saw their house increase in value by just under 10% in ten years.

If we compare the 10% real increase in inflation-adjusted market value with no mortgage, to the 311% total increase in home equity including both inflation and buying the home with an 80% loan to value (LTV) mortgage, then the real change in housing market values accounts for only 3% of the increase in home equity.

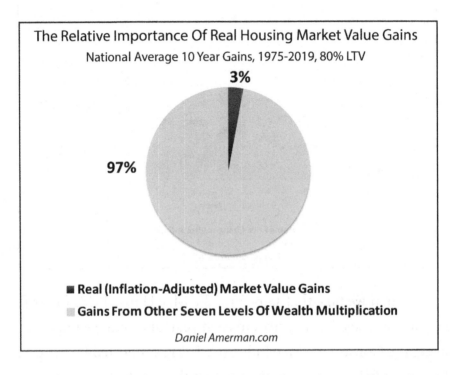

The Relative Importance Of Real Housing Market Value Gains
National Average 10 Year Gains, 1975-2019, 80% LTV

3%

97%

■ Real (Inflation-Adjusted) Market Value Gains
▨ Gains From Other Seven Levels Of Wealth Multiplication

Daniel Amerman.com

That's all. On a national average basis and over all the years, only 3% of the ten year increases in home equity have directly come from genuine increases in the inflation-adjusted value of the homes by themselves.

The other 97% all comes from the other seven levels of the multiplication of homeowner wealth.

Returning to our example from Book #1 of buying a $200,000 home using a $160,000 mortgage and $40,000 in starting home equity, the national average homeowner outcome was to see home equity grow to about $164,400 over ten years, an increase of $124,400.

If the homeowner had taken the same $40,000, and bought a smaller property or something else that went up by 10% in inflation-adjusted terms over ten years, with no inflation or mortgage, then they would have seen their equity go up by $4,000.

The $4,000 gain from the genuine increase in the market value not including inflation, is only 3% of the total $124,400 increase in home equity. To understand the source of the other $120,400 in additional net worth for the national average homeowner (or investor) over the decades - we need to understand the other seven layers of wealth multiplication, and their relationships with changes in real market value.

While the extensive historical research supporting this book is for the United States, the combination of inflation and mortgages has also created enormous wealth for homeowners in many other nations, and the same underlying wealth multiplication principles apply on a global basis.

This book is written primarily for homeowners - but everything also applies to investors who buy single family homes for rental purposes. Indeed, the research behind this book provides a uniquely in-depth look at how income property investors have historically built wealth over the decades. The dominant sources of equity gains have in practice actually been quite different than what many investors or potential investors believe.

The historical record is also quite clear that purchasing rental homes has on average over the decades produced both larger profits and more reliable profits than what is commonly understood - specifically because what is actually producing the profits and reliability is different from many people think. A better understanding of the actual underlying wealth creation engine allows for potentially much better investment decisions, whether the decision is about a home to live in or a home to rent out.

The Base For Three More Levels Of Multiplication

It is entirely accurate to say that the real change in inflation-adjusted values of homes - with no mortgage and no inflation - is directly responsible for only 3% of the average increase in home equity in ten years. However, it is not accurate to say that changes in inflation-adjusted home values are only responsible for 3% of home equity increases.

The difference is multiplication, or to be more specific - three more levels of the multiplication of wealth.

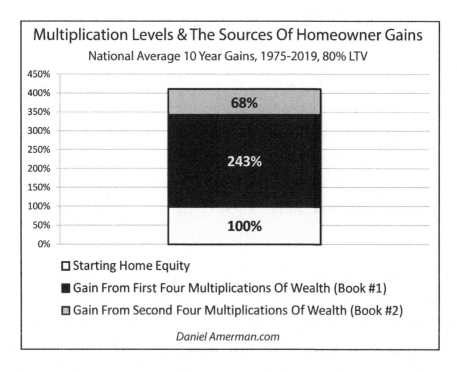

Book #1 covered the first four levels of wealth multiplication, and this Book #2 explores the second four levels of wealth multiplication. All four of these new levels of multiplication are based on changes in real market value - which is the fifth level of multiplication, if we are looking at all eight levels together.

As will be developed step by step in the following chapters, the sixth, seventh and eighth levels of the multiplication of homeowner wealth are the multiplicative relationships between real market value changes, and inflation, and the mortgage, and inflation and the mortgage in combination.

The national average homeowner experience over ten years is for these four levels to increase home equity by about 68% - so the additional levels of multiplication take the starting 10%

increase in real market values for homes, and amplify them by about 7X.

That seven times average amplification of real (inflation-adjusted) home price changes has been a tremendous source of net worth for average families over the decades, but it is only an average result for ten years. When we go beyond ten years, or look at times of higher inflation, then the amplification of real market value changes for the homeowners of the nation has been 10X, or 20X, or more.

One of the biggest differences between the first and second books is the reliability of the wealth creation. The first four levels of wealth multiplication are based on government policies (low to moderate inflation), government failures (high inflation), and the financial implications of the contractual relationship between the homeowner and the mortgage lender when we do have inflation. Put together, these factors not only account for the substantial majority of homeowner wealth creation over the decades, but they are also quite reliable over the years, they aren't really market forces or gambling or speculation.

On the other hand, changes in real home values are market based, they go up and they go down, and there has been a great deal of variation over the decades. However, because inflation dominates real home price changes over time, it can actually be hard to see whether real market changes have been positive or negative.

In the next chapter, we will use historical examples, show the huge range of real market value gains and losses, and demonstrate how they can be covered over by inflation. Using that information, we will then take a look at the historical 395 one to ten year homeownership experiences, and show just what the odds have been for real market values going up or down, for one year, four years and so forth.

In Chapters 3 & 4 we will develop the relationship between the base of real market home price changes and its multipliers, the sixth, seventh and eighth levels of the multiplication of wealth.

The financial implications of these repeated multiplications are fascinating but little understood. That is unfortunate, because these wealth multipliers have created vast amounts of net worth for homeowners and investors, particularly over longer periods of time. Indeed, when we take a look at a long time homeowner who has paid off their mortgage, and assume that they currently own a national average home that they bought decades before at the then national average price - then about $70,000 of their net worth is based just on the seventh and eighth levels of the multiplication of homeowner wealth.

In practice, something that most people aren't even aware exists, has through wealth multiplication created more net worth for older homeowners over the years, than the entire $65,000 median retirement account value (for the 50% of the population that has retirement accounts).

By the time all eight levels of the multiplication of homeowner wealth are put together, we have something amazing. The best way of creating wealth over time is the multiplication of wealth. Eight levels of multiplication are much more powerful than one level, and it is indeed all eight levels working together that explain why about half the net worth of two thirds of the population is found in their home equity.

However, there is also a problem that comes with this. The "problem" - which as problems go is a very good one to have - is that the increases in homeowner wealth are coming in from so many different directions that it becomes difficult to keep track of them all. The relative importance of the factors can vary quite a bit at different times, and for someone who is considering buying a home, whether to live in or as an investment, it is really helpful to be able to understand just where the gains have actually come from, and how reliable each of the sources have been.

Chapter 5 is devoted to the solution for the "problem" and that is the creation of a wealth map that visually shows the eight levels of the multiplication of wealth, with the surface area of each source showing its relative importance. For someone who bought an average home in 1975 with an 80% LTV mortgage, their home equity would have increased by 40 times by 2019 if they had experienced national average homeownership results. A wealth map is developed to visually show where every dollar of that remarkable forty-to-one increase actually came from.

Wealth maps and the eight levels of the multiplication of wealth are used for much shorter time periods in Chapter 6. Every component of the national average outcome of home equity almost doubling in the first three years of homeownership can now be clearly seen and understood, as well as the tripling in seven years and the quadrupling in ten years.

While the great majority of the American homeownership experience has been very positive - that has not always been true. Chapter 7 is entirely devoted to negative real market value changes, with a particular focus on the "worst of the worst", for those who bought homes near the peak of the housing bubble and were then hit by the financial crisis of 2008. The ability of the first four levels of wealth multiplication to effectively overpower real market value losses 80% of the time is also examined, as well as the 100% effectiveness in doing so on a national average basis for years not involving the peak of the bubble or the aftermath of the financial crisis.

Chapter 8 is all about the full details of eight different ways of "winning the lottery". Eight wealth maps show eight different ways the eight levels of the multiplication of wealth historically came together to produce a national average outcome of home equity increasing by about the original purchase price of the home, in just the first ten years of homeownership.

The final two chapters of the book take all that was learned through the intensive study of decades of information about how homeowner wealth was actually created in practice in the past, and use that information to explore some possibilities for the future.

Chapter 9 focuses on the inflationary dangers that are created by a very large national debt, and considers three scenarios for low, medium and high inflation that could end up being the result of the soaring national debts in the United States and other nations. The scenarios begin with looking at how higher rates of inflation benefit the government even while financially devastating savers.

Focusing just on inflation and the first four levels of the multiplication of wealth, the future wealth maps take that same information about the national debt, and show how to take that destruction of the value of savings and flip it into some of the most lucrative increases in home equity that we have ever experienced, as inflation is multiplied and turned into wealth. Indeed, assuming a 9% annual rate of inflation over the long term, we will track the exact dollars to map out how an eventual 92.5% destruction of the value of the dollar can be flipped into a 65 to 1 increase in home equity.

As established in Book 1 and further developed in this Book 2, *the historical evidence is overwhelming that owning a home with a mortgage is the single best defense against inflation that is available to the average person.* This is critical information for homeowners - and it is also critical information for investors who are concerned about the national debt and are seeking protection from inflation.

Chapter 10 adds in the factors of a growing population, as well as very low interest rates and the increasing concentration and density of population in some areas of the country. If these long term trends increase real market values over the coming decades at the same time that the national debt is sending inflation rates jumping upwards - then there is a multiplication of a multiplication that reverberates through the levels of the multiplication of wealth.

This effective multiplication of the impact of the growth in the national debt times the impact of the growth in population has the potential to set off an upwards explosion in homeowner equity. As can be seen in the final wealth map, the second and third levels of wealth multiplication from Book 1 combine with the seventh and eighth levels of wealth multiplication from this Book 2, and those four wealth multipliers all acting together could create what would be by far the largest profits for homeowners (and investors) that we have ever seen, with $45,000 becoming $4.5 million over the long term in the final scenario. This could make the buy-versus-rent decision the single most important financial decision of a lifetime, perhaps making the difference between prosperity and poverty for millions of people.

Before we get to the eight ways the homeowner "lottery" has been won in the past, or mapping out the dollar mechanics of how a soaring national debt can create explosive increases in home equity in the future, we need to first develop and understand the fifth through eighth levels of the multiplication of homeowner wealth. We will start in the next chapter by learning how to see through an illusion that fools most homeowners (and most investors too).

Chapter 2

Home Price Changes That Are Not From Inflation

As we explored in Book 1, home prices are dominated by inflation over the long term.

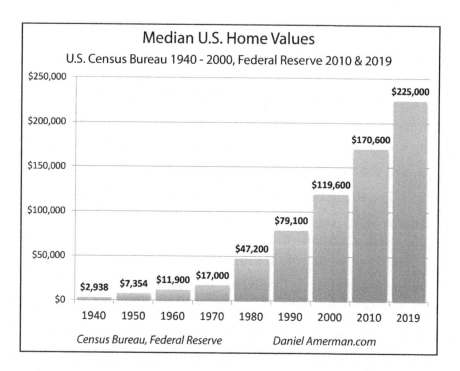

The doubling and doubling of the dollars needed to buy most things - including homes - in a formula that is the same as the compound interest formula does explain most of why median home values have so reliably increased over the decades.

However, not all changes in home prices are based on inflation. The housing market does go up and down. The shorter the time period, or the lower the rate of inflation, then the more important that changes in the housing market become. This is particularly true when we move away from national averages, and look at specific cities, neighborhoods or homes.

Seeing Real Changes In Market Value

To understand real changes in the market values of homes we need to first know how to see them.

An example of homes almost exactly keeping up with inflation can be found in the six years between 1992 and 1998. Using the Federal Reserve median home value of $225,000 from 2019, and then adjusting the prices with the Freddie Mac House Price Index, the national average home price for a comparable home was $83,376 in 1992, and $97,189 in 1998.

The normal way of looking at this and the way almost all homeowners would see this is that they had a $13,813 gain, which was about 16.6% in six years. On a national average basis, homeowners who bought with 20% down or $16,675 in 1992, would have seen that equity increase to $30,488, which was a gain of 83% in just six years even without including mortgage amortization. (The home equity gain including amortization was 106%, a little more than doubling the equity.)

All of that $13,813 home price gain was an absolutely real increase in net worth, as real as any other kind of money.

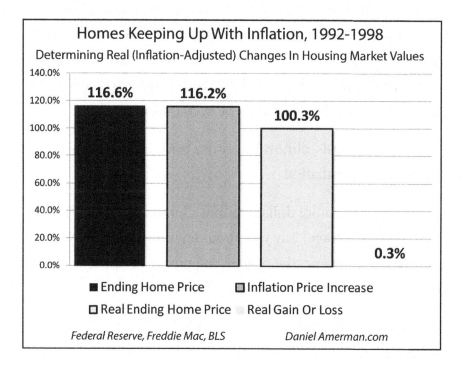

However, because of six years of low to moderate inflation, it took 16.2% more dollars to buy most things by 1998, meaning that it took $116.20 to buy what $100 would have paid for in 1992. If we compare the two left bars in the graph above, the increase in the number of dollars to buy an average home was almost exactly equal to the increase in the number of dollars needed to buy almost anything else.

If we take the $97,189 home price in 1998, and divide it by the increased number of dollars it took to pay for everything, then

$97,189 / 1.162 = \$83,639$, which is 100.3% of the starting home price of \$83,376.

When we divide the ending home price (the first bar) by the increase in the Consumer Price Index, the increase in dollars needed to buy things as a result of inflation (the second bar), we get the real market value of the house in 1998 in inflation-adjusted terms (the third bar). That is almost identical to the purchase price of the home in 1992, with just a miniscule 0.3% gain that is so small it can't even be seen on the graph.

In other words, almost the entire price increase was just keeping up with inflation.

It took 16% more dollars to buy a home. It took 16% more dollars to (on average) buy just about anything else as well. The real value of the home, the purchasing power of the dollars it took to buy or sell the home was essentially unchanged.

Now, keeping up with inflation is a whole lot better than not keeping up with inflation. However, homeowners without mortgages would have just broken even when it comes not to the amount of dollars their home would sell for, but what those dollars would buy for them.

Real Gains In Home Market Values

To see an example of a real housing market gain, let's look at the years 2012 to 2018. Based on the combination of the

Federal Reserve and Freddie Mac numbers, a national average home would have cost $145,340 in 2012, and the same home would have cost $216,398 in 2018. The national average was a homeowner gain of $71,058, or 48.9%.

For the average homeowner who bought in 2012 with a 20% starting equity of $29,068, even without amortization they would have seen that equity increase to just over $100,000, meaning they would have more than tripled their home equity in six years.

Again, the $71,058 gain was entirely real and spendable money, and the way most people see the world - that is all there is to it, an over $71,000 gain on a $29,000 cash down payment in just six years.

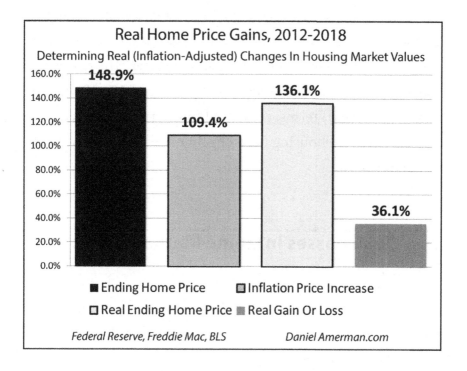

However, there was inflation in each of those six years as well, and it increased the number of dollars needed to buy most things by 109.4%, so that it took $109.40 in 2018 to pay for what $100 would have purchased in 2012.

When we compare the heights of the two bars on the left - the increase in home prices was much greater than what could be explained by inflation. There was clearly a very real and major increase in homeowner wealth for the nation that went well beyond just keeping up with inflation.

To calculate the size of the real gain in housing market values for the nation between 2012 and 2018 - we need to get rid of inflation. We do this in the same way that we did for the break even example: we divide the first bar of ending home price increases by the second bar of inflation price increases, and that gives us the third bar of real ending home prices. The national average for 2018 was for home prices to be up to 136.1% in real (inflation-adjusted) terms, compared to where they started in 2012. This is a real housing market gain of 36.1%, as shown with the fourth bar.

Real Losses In Home Market Values

There was what appeared to be a very similar 46.5% six year gain in housing market values for the nation that occurred between 1978 and 1984.

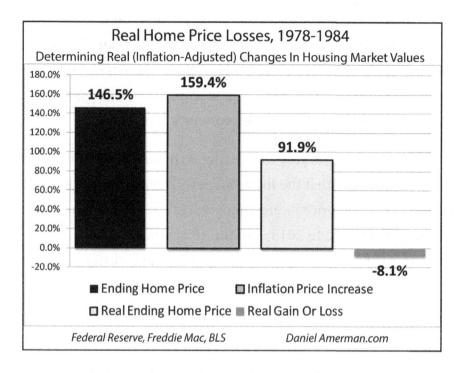

However, those were not years of low inflation but of high inflation. Comparing the heights of the two left bars, the increases in prices as a result of inflation are now higher than the increase in home prices. This means that the homeowners of the nation actually lost money in terms of the market values of their homes, when we look not just at dollars but at what dollars will buy, the purchasing power of their homes. They failed to keep up with inflation.

To find the amount of the real loss - we repeat the same steps. We start with the first bar of homes costing 146.5% more. We divide by the second bar of it taking 159.4% more dollars to just keep up with inflation. This means that real home prices in purchasing power terms actually fell by 1984, to being only 91.9% of where they were in 1978, as shown with the third bar.

In practice, the homeowners of the nation on average lost 8.1% of the real value of their home over the six years. (Or, at least they would have if they owned their homes with no mortgages. With mortgages and the nine high stacking they still made a lot of money as will be explored in the coming chapters.)

Where this gets very interesting is that the way most people see the world and that the financial news is usually reported - the changes in home prices were almost identical between the 48.9% increase from 2012 to 2018, and the 46.5% increase between 1978 and 1984. Yet, when it comes to financial security and what money will buy - the actual experience for the nation was one of radically different outcomes, it was the difference between gaining 36% and losing 8%.

This is the fifth level of the multiplication of wealth, the multiplication of home prices that is the result of real housing market gains (or losses).

If being able to see the difference between gaining 36% and losing 8% in purchasing power is important - and it should be - *then it is mandatory to look at inflation-adjusted dollars and real market value changes.* This is why the use of real dollars is quite common with more upper level financial and investment analysis, and why they are much more extensively used in my somewhat more sophisticated materials on real estate investment than they are in this book on owning a home.

However, the general public is not usually shown information in this way, and most people are not aware of this enormously important foundation principle for investing, which is how the destruction of the value of money has historically often concealed the destruction of the value of savings and investments. This has historically included some long historical periods of fairly devastating and long term losses with both stocks and precious metals, that most people are simply not aware of.

For homeowners, the important lesson here is that real housing market losses do occur, and they are much more common than most people have any idea. The reason that people are not aware is that real losses don't look like ordinary losses - because the great majority of the time, the price of the home is going up, just not as fast as the rate of inflation. The ongoing compounded increase in the number of dollars that it takes to buy almost everything - including homes - is so strong and so relentless that it papers over many of the real fluctuations in value in the housing market.

Changes In The Housing Market

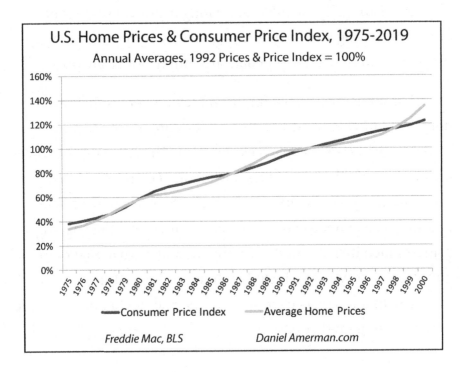

It is also worth noting that the housing market and its relationship with inflation changed around the year 2000. There has historically been a strong relationship between inflation and housing prices, and the match between the two used to be remarkably close.

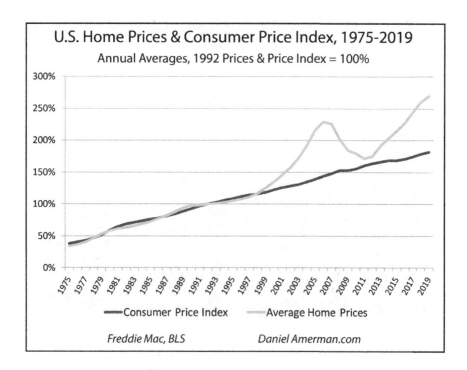

However, since the year 2000 or so - the relationship between inflation and housing prices has not been as tight as it used to be.

We saw by far the largest increase in housing prices over the rate of inflation with the expansion of the housing bubble in the early 2000s. We saw by far the largest decrease in home prices for any reasons in the years 2007 through 2011 in particular. Since that time, national average home prices have again been increasing at a rate that is well above what the government says is the rate of inflation.

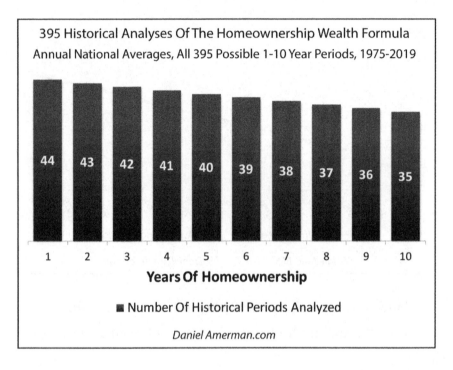

Average Real Home Price Changes Over 1-10 Year Periods

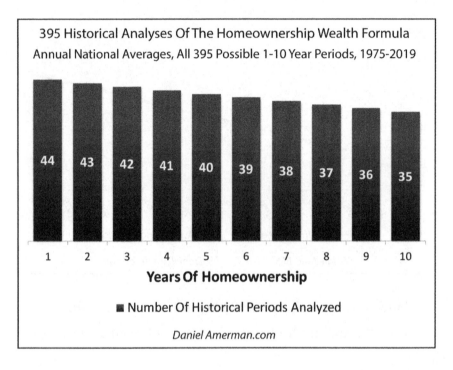

To break out what actual homeowner experiences have been with real home price changes, we need to return to our 395 possible 1-10 year homeownership periods between 1975 and 2019.

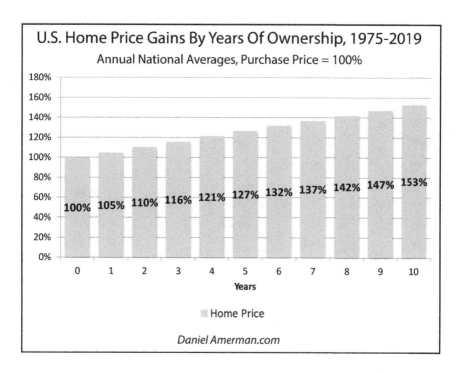

We start by looking at total price changes - including both inflation and what wasn't inflation.

Averaging together all 44 of the possible 1 year homeownership periods, the average homeowner saw the price of their home rise by 5% in that year. Looking at 5 year homeownership periods, the average home rose 27% in value, and with the 10 year homeownership periods, the total average increase in price was 53%.

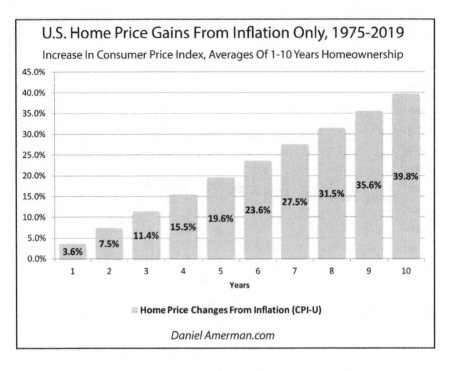

We then use the same formula developed earlier in this chapter for separating real home price changes from inflation. Take the increase in home prices, divide by the increase in the number of dollars it takes to buy everything (as measured by the consumer price index), and we find the national homeownership experience when it comes to real value changes in the housing market.

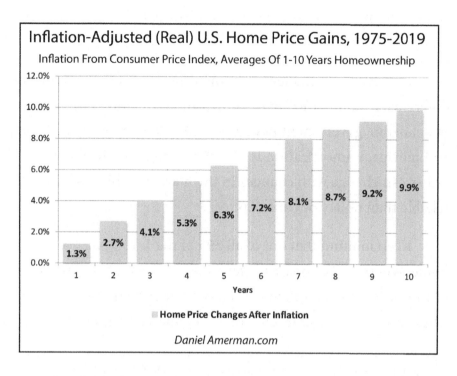

Inflation-Adjusted (Real) U.S. Home Price Gains, 1975-2019

Inflation From Consumer Price Index, Averages Of 1-10 Years Homeownership

Home Price Changes After Inflation

Daniel Amerman.com

If we look three years out, the average of all the 42 possible three year homeownership periods was for home prices to climb by 16%, while the average of the 42 increases in price from inflation was 11.4%. If we divide 116% by 111.4%, the national average homeownership experience was to see the real, inflation-adjusted market value of their home climb by 4.1% in their first three years, as shown in the graph above. (The actual numbers behind the graph are based on averaging 42 different real price gains, which is a different methodology, but the results of 4.1% are the same in this case.)

Using the same formula, for all the possible 1 year homeownership periods, the average was for homes to increase by 1.3% in value in the first year, not including inflation. This national average increase rose to a real 6.3% gain over the first five years of homeownership, and about a 10% gain over the first ten years.

However, real changes in home value have a very important difference from inflation and amortization. Inflation is a matter of deliberate government policy, at least at low to moderate levels, and mortgage amortization is a matter of contract. Real home prices can change with changes in the market - which is far less reliable than policy or contracts.

Keep in mind that out of all 395 of the 1-10 year homeownership periods, as determined in Book 1 there was only one negative when looking at inflation only, and no negatives when looking at the combination of inflation and amortization.

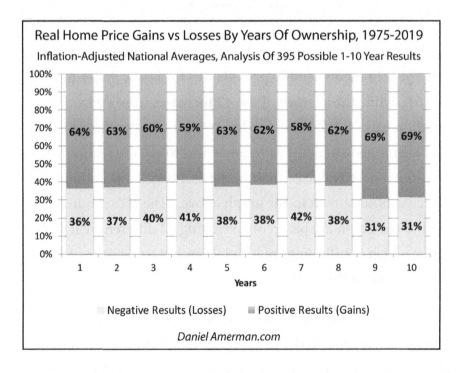

However, when we include changes in real home values, which includes changes in the real estate market and fluctuations in supply and demand across the nation - then a great deal of volatility is introduced. Out of the 44 possible one year homeownership periods - homeowners had negative results in 16 of them. So what the nation experienced was a 36% chance that the real value of their home fell in the first year they owned it. (*This is not the same thing as their actual home price falling*, which was much less likely because of the shield that is provided by inflation.)

When we separate home values from inflation, looking only at changes in purchasing power, then there was a 41% chance that real home values would fall over four years of home ownership (17 negative outcomes out of 41 possibilities).

When we went out to ten years with inflation only - then we got a great deal of cushion from the one way process of inflation, the one year and two year outliers fell away and were smoothed out by the steady, cumulative destruction of the value of the dollar. However, with real home values, not including inflation - going out ten years helps, but not as much as one might think. Even with a full ten years going by, our real changes in home values were still negative 31% of the time (11 negative price changes out of 35 possible ten year homeownership periods).

On average, changes in real home prices are a *positive*. When we look at all 395 of the 1-10 year homeownership possibilities, there were 247 times that the change in real home values was positive. This means that 63% of the time - the homeowner not only benefited, but they benefited from the

positive multiplication of the multiplication. As we will explore
in the next few chapters, when this average result of a positive
multiplication of a multiplication is then stacked five high
- the result for the average homeowner over the decades of
including real price changes has been to add another layer of the
multiplication of wealth, to the substantial personal advantage of
all those tens of millions of households.

That said, including real home price changes very much
adds a "wild card" to our previously quite reliable mix. A 37%
chance of a loss (in inflation-adjusted terms) is very real, and can
have major consequences, as many people found out in the 2007
to 2011 period (as explored in much more detail in Chapter 7).

Now, a 63% historical chance of "winning" is actually
pretty good, much better than what we would see with a casino
or lottery. To have a 63% chance of a positive inflation-adjusted
outcome over all the historical 1-10 year holding periods might
be considered in some ways to be similar to investing in stocks.
The average outcome is very good, but particularly over the short
and medium term - there are no guarantees.

Chapter 3

Multiplying Real Home Price Gains Times Inflation For Reliable Profits

In Book 1 and in the previous chapters, we developed two primary sources of home price changes, those of inflation gains and real market value gains.

In this chapter we will combine those two primary sources, but we won't add them - we will instead multiply them. And what we will find is that when we multiply - the product is indeed greater than the sum of the parts, and the implications for wealth creation are quite powerful.

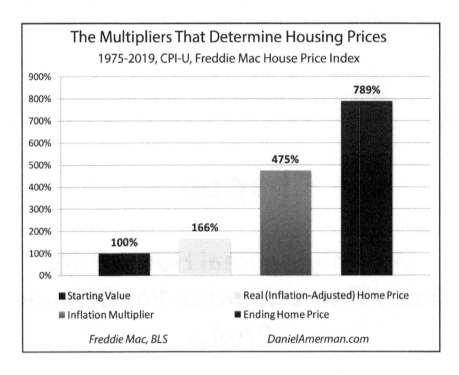

The Multipliers That Determine Housing Prices
1975-2019, CPI-U, Freddie Mac House Price Index

Based on the Freddie Mac Home Price Index, the average home in the United States had a value in 2019 that was equal to 789% of its value in 1975, and this can be seen in the "Ending Home Price" bar on the right. As developed in Book 1 and based on national averages, a home that sold for $28,500 in 1975 would have sold for $225,000 in 2019. Keep in mind that this is for equivalent homes, with the same size, amenities and average metro area locations.

The Consumer Price Index, the cost of paying for a standard of living for an average urban consumer, rose from 53.8 in 1975, to about 255.7 in 2019. This is an increase of 375%, meaning it would take (on average) $4.75 to pay for what would have cost $1.00 in 1975, as shown with the "Inflation Multiplier" bar.

When we take the changing value of a dollar into account, which is also known as using *real* or *inflation-adjusted dollars*, then a $28,500 home rose to a real value of $47,400. This was a real gain of $18,900, which is a 66% gain over the starting price, and that is shown in the "Real (Inflation-Adjusted) Home Price" bar. This is the fifth level of the multiplication of wealth.

This type of graph applies to a lot more than just home prices. Anytime we have gains or other changes in price, particularly over long periods of time, we have two sources of price changes. One source is dollars that represent real increases in value, and the other is just having lots more dollars, because dollars are worth much less, and it takes a lot more dollars to buy just about anything.

To get the number of dollars to buy a home in the future - or anything else - we take the new real value of the home (or stocks or gold or bonds), and *multiply* it times how many more dollars it takes to buy just about anything, due to inflation. Now, because inflation increases prices using the compound interest formula, that effectively means we multiply real gains times the compound interest formula, and this generates *a lot of headlines* over the years for "record" prices, whether we are looking at stocks, real estate, gold, art or collectibles.

For the 1975 to 2019 period, we start with a home value of 100%, we *multiply* times 166% for the real (or inflation-adjusted) national average change in home values, and we then *multiply again* times 475% - because it takes $4.75 to buy what used to cost a dollar. We end up with a home that is worth 789% of where we started.

Restated, we start with a $28,500 home, we *multiply* times 166% to get a real home value of $47,400, then we *multiply a second time*, times 475% to take inflation into account, and we end up with a $225,000 home, 44 years later.

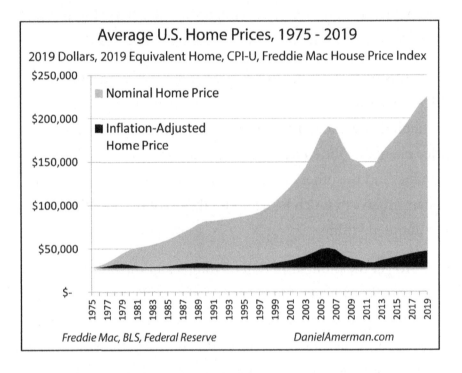

Average U.S. Home Prices, 1975 - 2019
2019 Dollars, 2019 Equivalent Home, CPI-U, Freddie Mac House Price Index

Freddie Mac, BLS, Federal Reserve   DanielAmerman.com

The longer the time period, the more important that inflation becomes, and the more important the double multiplication. So a $18,900 real gain grows to a $196,500 total gain, of which $177,600 is based on inflation, and on the multiplication of the increase in the number of dollars that it takes to buy just about anything.

The Multiplication Of Real Gains & Inflation

Crucially, however, saying that the $177,600 home price difference is due to inflation is not the same thing as saying that inflation by itself accounted for $177,600 of home price gains. Inflation increased the number of dollars needed to buy most things up to 475% of the starting price. So, if we take a starting price of $28,500 and multiply it times 475%, then we get a home price of $135,400 - which is an increase of a little over $106,900.

If we just add together the $18,900 real gain, and the $106,900 price increase solely from inflation, then we have $125,800 in combined gains - which is $70,700 short of the $196,500 actual total gain.

Where did the extra $70,700 come from?

Let me suggest that this is a fairly important question. The mystery $70,700 is almost four times as much as the $18,900 in real price gains. It is also about 2.5 times as much as the original purchase price of the home.

The source of the extra $70,700 takes us back to the very heart of reliable wealth creation over the long term and that is that we aren't adding the gains, we are *multiplying the gains*.

For a round number example to understand where the extra money came from, let's consider two primary sources of wealth, two investments, each of which quadruples our money over time. If they are entirely separate investments, then $1 becomes $4 from one source of wealth, and the other $1 becomes $4 from the second investment. We made two $1 investments, and ended up with $4 plus $4, or $8 dollars. We are adding two multiplicative sources of wealth, and the results are not bad at all.

Now let's change the rules and say that we made a single investment, and that it was multiplicative. First we made four times the money. And then we made four times that money again. Instead of adding $4 to $4 - we multiply $4 times $4 - and we get $16.

Those are round numbers, but that is the basic relationship. Four plus four is eight, but four times four is sixteen - there is an "extra" eight due to the multiplication. That basic mathematical relationship is also what happens when we have two primary sources for future home prices, the wealth drivers of inflation and real price gains. To combine inflation and real price gains, we don't add them like we would four plus four, but we multiply them like we would four times four. To determine future home prices, we multiply real market gains times inflation gains.

A house becomes fundamentally more valuable. There could be less available building space near a city, or a neighborhood becomes trendier to live in, or there may be a fixed supply of lakefront or oceanfront properties. Whatever the source or sources, people are willing to pay more for the house, its real market value is climbing.

At the same time, inflation is occurring and growing over time with the power of compound interest. It takes more dollars to buy anything and everything.

So we take the real increase in the value of the home, we multiply it by the increase in the dollars it takes to buy everything, and we get an additional level of wealth that goes beyond the sum of the parts, more than can be explained by just real market gains or just inflation gains.

This is the seventh level of the multiplication of wealth: the multiplication of real housing market gains by compounded inflation gains.

This multiplication can be seen visually in the first graph by comparing the heights of the bars for "Real (Inflation-Adjusted) Home Price", "Inflation Multiplier" and "Ending Home Price". The "Inflation Multiplier" bar of 475% towers over the "Real Home Price" bar of 166%. But yet, when we combine the bars, we get the "Ending Home Price" bar of 789% that seems disproportionately large, if all we are doing is adding in that little "Real Home Price" bar.

The explanation for the height of the final bar is that we are not adding the bars, *but multiplying the bars.* We take the new housing price of 166% of the starting housing price (100% start + 66% real gain) and we *multiply* it times the new number of dollars that are 475% of what they used to be (100% start + 375% inflation gain), to get to the 789% ending home price.

In dollar terms, the starting home price was $28,500. The real gain was 66%, or $18,900. The inflation gain on the starting home price was 375%, or $106,900. *Because the real gain is not added to the inflation gain, but multiplied, we also get a 375% inflation gain on the 66% real price gain, and this creates a 248% gain that is worth $70,700.*

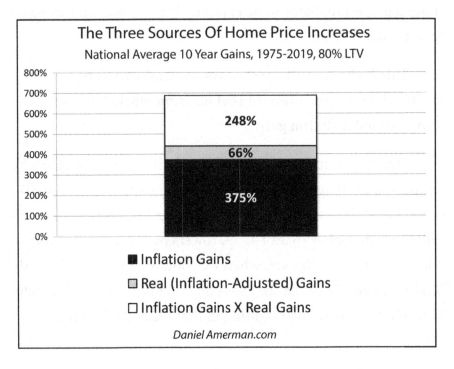

The sum of the 66% real gain, the 375% inflation gain, and the 248% real gain times inflation gain, is equal to 689%, which when combined with the 100% starting home value, entirely accounts for the national average 789% home price gain between 1975 and 2019.

The multiplication of two sources of wealth is worth far more than the addition of two sources of wealth. Homes have gotten steadily more valuable in real terms over the decades as the population has grown, low interest rates have made mortgage payments more affordable, and in many areas, the combination of a shrinking supply of available land and growing regulatory burdens have limited the supply of new housing. That has created wealth for those who own homes.

At the same time, the government has been pursuing highly reliable and consistent policies of trying to make sure it takes more dollars to buy things each year than it did the year before - including homes. Over the decades, the dollars it takes to buy homes has increased with the full power of the compound interest formula, accounting for the great majority of national home price increases.

We take decades of real home prices climbing and multiply that times decades of inflation growing prices with the power of compound interest, and an explosion of sorts occurs with that multiplication of wealth.

Starting Home Price = $28,500

Primary real price gain = 66% X $28,500 = $18,900

Primary inflation gain = 375% X $28,500 = $106,900

"Extra" real price times inflation gain = 66% X 375% X $28,500 = $70,700

Ending Home Price = $28,500 + $18,900 + $106,900 + $70,700 = $225,000

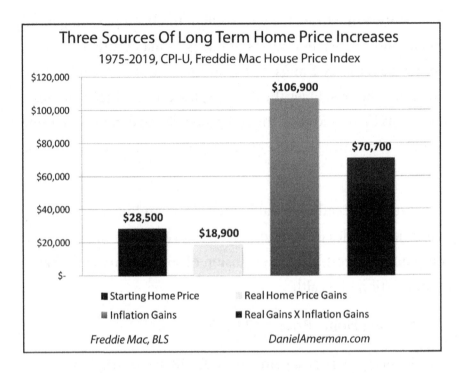

Over the long term, 1975-2019, the median U.S. home value went from $28,500 to $225,000. Of that $18,900 were real market gains by themselves, $106,900 was inflation by itself, and $70,700 was "boom", the extra level of wealth creation that is the product of multiplying two primary wealth sources times each other.

Because this "extra" level is the secondary multiplication of the two underlying primary multiplications of real gains and inflation gains, it has some special characteristics. The first is that because it is the multiplication of two multiplications, it is acutely sensitive to changes in either of the underlying multiplications.

If real home price gains were zero - then multiplying times real home price gains would lead to zero, and the only source of gains would be the $106,900 inflation gains. If inflation gains were zero, then multiplying times inflation gains would lead to zero, and the only source of gains would be the $18,900 real home price gains.

However, another special characteristic of wealth coming from the multiplication of two multiplications is that if both underlying sources are there and both are significant - then there can be an almost explosive increase in home price as a result, to an extent that might seem counterintuitive to many people. The "Real Gains X Inflation Gains" bar does indeed completely tower over both the "Starting Home Price" and "Real Home Price Gains" bars.

As we will develop in the following chapters, what is the most important feature of this multiplication of multiplications, is that it then sets the stage for another round of the multiplication of wealth (as developed in Book 1) when a home is bought with a mortgage.

When all these levels of successive multiplications are combined, the result might be starting to seem a little technical, or obscure. But here is what matters: *this wealth creation is entirely real and it has historically been massive.* If we look at the actual total wealth creation for the whole of the two thirds of the population that are homeowners, and we look at long homeownership periods, then this multiplication of the multiplications has created vastly more real world wealth than the sum of the wealth created from all of the day trading, or technical charting, or wave analysis, or house flipping, or stock speculation, or options speculation combined.

And as we will explore in Chapter Ten, if the future is indeed one of both significant inflation and long term real home price increases, then this seemingly obscure series of multiplications is likely to again become one of the largest sources of wealth creation for the nation over the long term, dwarfing the combined results from many of the intentional and *seemingly* much more sophisticated investment strategies that will be deployed over the coming years. (From a financial engineering perspective, the specifics of how a home with a mortgage creates wealth is actually more sophisticated than the great majority of consumer investment strategies.)

Now, if almost no one out of the tens of millions of households who owned homes over multiple decades had thought through the mathematics of the multiplication of real prices times inflation and how it was increasing their personal household net worth by tens of thousands of dollars over the decades - that didn't matter in the slightest. They still got the potentially huge increase in net worth, or the money if they sold.

The Homeowner Wealth Formula is a natural flow of wealth, there was no need to understand every component of what was happening - or even any of the components - in order for a nation of homeowners to fully benefit from the flow of wealth, and in this case, the somewhat obscure but lucrative multiplication of the multiplications of wealth.

Seeing The Sources Of Wealth Creation

In the earlier bar graph, we multiplied 166% for the real (inflation-adjusted) home price times 475% because of inflation growing inside the compound interest formula, and produced a combined result of the total home price climbing to 789% of its starting price. That same multiplication can be done for any other time period, and the next graph shows the annual factors for real price gains and inflation, as well as their multiplication in each year to get the actual home price changes in simple (nominal) dollars.

For instance, if we look at 1975 to 1990, then real price gains were 18%, inflation gains were 143%, and when we multiply 118% times 243% we get a total home price in 1990 that is up to 287% of where it started.

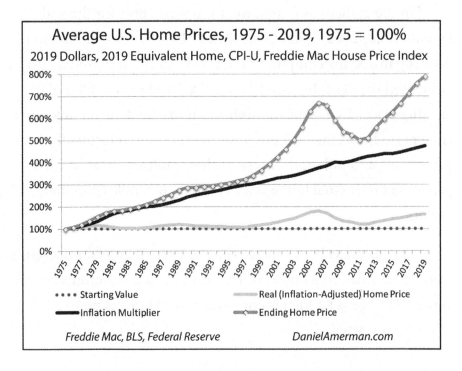

Average U.S. Home Prices, 1975 - 2019, 1975 = 100%

2019 Dollars, 2019 Equivalent Home, CPI-U, Freddie Mac House Price Index

Legend:
•••• Starting Value   Real (Inflation-Adjusted) Home Price
—— Inflation Multiplier   Ending Home Price

Freddie Mac, BLS, Federal Reserve   *DanielAmerman.com*

What is illustrated in this one graph - *if properly understood* - can be the solid foundation for a lifetime of building financial security, whether it be through homeownership or investing in income properties. The sources of wealth creation and the relationships between them are worthy of close and even repeated study, as they have created enormous amounts of wealth in the past, across the decades and in many nations.

In analyzing this crucial graph, the following are some particularly important points to keep in mind.

1) *See the visual dominance of inflation over time.* Many people might argue that this series was written in backwards order, with the first book being devoted to seemingly technical factors like inflation and the compound interest formula, with

what everyone knows is the real money-making "sizzle" of market value changes not even appearing until the second book.

As common as that perception might be - the actual historical evidence is overwhelming that over time inflation is far more important when it comes to building homeowner wealth. The long term, one way and cumulative process of it taking ever more money each year to buy things, particularly when compounded inside the compound interest formula, completely overwhelms real market value changes by themselves.

2. *Study the relationships between the Real (Inflation-Adjusted) Home Price line, the Inflation Multiplier line and the Ending Home Price line over time.* Those relationships are the heart of it all, the core sources of homeowner and investor profits.

The Real Home Price line is by itself trivial when compared to the other two lines. What matters most is not that line by itself - but its multiplicative relationship with the Inflation Multiplier line. Whenever the Real Home Price line rises significantly above the base 100% starting line, opening up even a narrow visual gap, the same gap appears above it, as a wider gap opens between the Inflation Multiplier line and the Ending Home Price line.

3. *See the seventh level of the multiplication of homeowner wealth.* As can easily be seen visually, the surface area of the gap between the two top lines is often much larger than what would be produced by just adding the Real Home Price and Inflation Multiplier lines. The additional increase in home prices is the seventh level, and because it is a multiplication, it is acutely sensitive to changes in either of the underlying factors. Whenever

there is a combination of substantial cumulative inflation, and then there are real market gains, the multiplication of those two creates a vast increase in the surface area of wealth, much greater than the underlying real market value changes. The farther out we go in time, and the greater the cumulative inflation, the more explosive the total price increase that is produced from a given 10%, or 20%, or 30% increase in real market values.

4. *Keep the mortgage and the five high stacking in mind.* As developed in Book 1 of this series, the third level of the multiplication of homeowner wealth is turning inflation into wealth via the multiplication of inflation gains when a home is bought with a mortgage. As will be developed in the next two chapters in particular, that same multiplication also applies to the fifth and seventh levels of homeowner wealth multiplication, real price gains and the multiplication of real price gains times inflation.

So, it isn't just the lines in the previous graph that matter - it is the multiplication of each of the lines times five when a home is acquired with an 80% LTV mortgage. When we look at the explosion upwards in surface area when inflation is multiplied times real price gains, and then we multiply that product times five again because the home was bought with a mortgage, the result is a massive increase in the dollars of new home equity, relative to the starting home equity investment.

5. *See the tilted amplification of the underlying real gains.* This step is critical when it comes to the reliability and magnitude of wealth creation, and it is something that really sets this category of investments apart from many others. As can be

readily seen, while the top line of Ending Home Prices tends to mirror big moves up and down with the underlying Real Home Prices line, the shapes and the slopes of the lines are not the same.

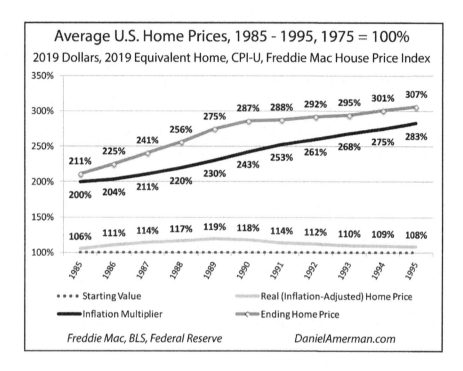

An early example can be seen in the graph above, when we zoom in to just the years 1985 to 1995. Real (inflation-adjusted) Home Prices rose from 106% in 1985, to a peak of 119% in 1989, and then fell back to 108% by 1995. For each year, the Ending Home Price line is determined by simply multiplying the Real Home Price line by the Inflation Multiplier line, and when we multiply 106% times 200% in 1985, we get the 211% Ending Home Price line.

As the underlying Real Home Prices climb from 106% to 119%, then Ending Home Prices also jumped upwards, *but much faster*, from 211% to 275%. The reason is that the Inflation

Multiplier line is climbing at the same time as the Real Home Price line, and we are not adding those two lines, but multiplying them. Real Home Prices rose by 13%, the Inflation Multiplier rose by 40%, but their multiplied product rose by 64%.

In 1990, Real Home Prices fell, and they fell for the next 5 years, meaning that Real Home Prices fell in 6 out of the 11 years shown. Ending Home Prices did not fall, however, but rather they increased for 11 out of the 11 years. The reason is that the increases in the Inflation Multiplier line overwhelmed the fall in the Real Home Prices line, *as is usually the case* (there is much more on this in Chapter 7).

The Ending Home Price line went from 275% in 1989 to 287% in 1990, despite the Real Home Price line declining from 119% to 118%, and the reason was that the Inflation Multiplier line climbed from 230% to 243%.

If we look at 1995, then Real Home Prices had completed a round trip of sorts, cycling up from 106% to a peak of 119% in four years, and then cycling back down to 108% over the next six years. These up and down cycles are quite common with most investment categories, particularly when we look in inflation-adjusted terms.

However, Ending Home Prices did not cycle up and down, but rather went up and up for the full 11 years, climbing from 211% to 307%. This was an almost 50% gain - because of the almost 50% gain in the Inflation Multiplier line. So, the relationship between the lines is not just an amplification of increases in the Real Home Price line, but a change in the slope as well, where the gains are there in full and in multiplied form, but the losses are (usually) overcome, *leading to the extraordinary result of multiplied upside and no downside. With that extraordinary result then being multiplied again because of the power of the mortgage.*

That is an amazingly powerful and reliable literal formula for building wealth - and it is also just the natural byproduct of borrowing the money to buy a four bedroom house in the suburbs, and then living a life, while giving the compound interest formula and the multiplication of compound interest (in the form of inflation) the years needed to work their magic.

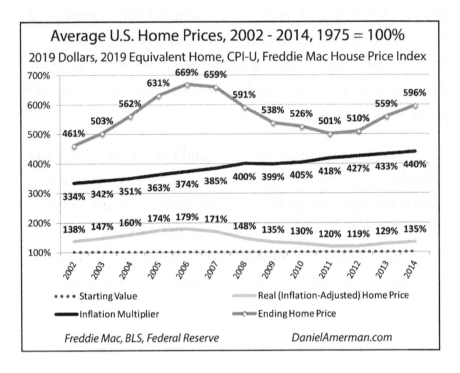

This same relationship can also be seen when we focus on the years 2002, 2009 and 2014 in the graph above. When we look at Real Home Prices, they cycled up from 2002 to a peak in 2006, then cycled down to a trough in 2012, and then cycled back up in another up cycle that has persisted through the writing of this book. Along the way, real home prices hit about the 135% mark three times, including 138% in 2002, 135% in 2009 and 135% in 2014.

As covered in much more detail in Chapter 7, what was very unusual about this period is that there were actual and major decreases in Ending Home Prices in some years. That said, we can still see both the tilt and the amplification when we compare Ending Home Prices to Real Home Prices in 2002, 2009 and 2014.

Real Home Prices started at 138%, went way up, and then came all the way back down to 135% by 2009. Ending Home Prices started at 461%, but did not cycle all the way back down, and were still up at 538% in 2009 - because the Inflation Multiplier line had climbed from 334% to 399%.

Real Home Prices were very slightly lower by 2014 than what they had been in 2002, when we take out inflation the market was still down a bit after twelve years. However, when we do include the Inflation Multiplier line climbing from 334% to 440%, and multiply the Real Home Price line times that line, then we get Ending Home Prices that increased from 461% to 596%. When it came to the multiplication of wealth, it was that increase that was then multiplied by the power of the mortgage to create a great deal of increased wealth from what was actually an almost flat market in real terms.

Inflation and the mortgage combine to give the homeowner (or investor) an almost unfair advantage, where real gains are multiplied upwards for truly extraordinary results, flat markets are turned into still substantial wealth, and even down markets are either avoided altogether (usually), or greatly reduced.

As we will review in Chapters 4 & 5, this "unfair advantage" has historically created extraordinary wealth for generations of homeowners. As we will explore in Chapter 10, these relationships and the multiplications of the multiplications may lead to historically unprecedented future homeowner profits, if the higher inflation resulting from a soaring national debt is multiplied by the higher home prices that can be associated with a growing population.

The sources of what could be the single best financial opportunity of their lifetimes for many people in the future, can be understood by studying the lines of the past - if we know what to look for.

Chapter 4

The History Of Eight Levels Of The Multiplication Of Wealth

Financial history makes it crystal clear that multiplying wealth over the long term is a much more powerful force than simply adding wealth. When we look at the specific history of homeownership in the United States, it is the process of multiplication and the compound interest formula that has created so much wealth for so many millions of households over the decades.

In Book 1 of this series, *"The Homeowner Wealth Formula"*, we developed the first four levels of wealth multiplications. They are:

1) The multiplication of the dollars needed to buy homes with each year of inflation;

2) The multiplication of the multiplications that occurs with inflation over multiple years, as home prices climb over time with the power of the compound interest formula;

3) The multiplication and five high stacking that occurs with compounded inflation gains relative to home equity when a home is purchased with a mortgage; and

4) The multiplication and four high stacking that occurs with amortization increases in equity when a home is purchased with a mortgage.

In Chapters 2 & 3 of this second book, we added the fifth and seventh levels of the multiplication of wealth. In this chapter we add the final two levels, the sixth and eighth levels, to get all of the second four levels:

5) The multiplication of home prices that is the result of real housing market gains (or losses);

6) The multiplication and five high stacking that occurs with real market gains relative to home equity when a home is purchased with a mortgage;

7) The multiplication of real housing market gains by compounded inflation gains; and

8) The multiplication and five high stacking that occurs relative to home equity as the result of the multiplication of real market gains by compounded inflation gains, when a home is purchased with a mortgage.

Eight Levels Of Multiplication Over The Long Term

To see how all eight levels of multiplication work with the Homeowner Wealth Formula, let's take the long term numbers from 1975 to 2019. That is a long period of time - but it is also easily compatible with a single lifetime. Let's say that an average person bought a home in 1975 at age 25 with an 80% LTV mortgage, that they owned the same home at age 69 in 2019, and that they experienced the exactly average increase in home prices for the nation.

The Federal Reserve Survey of Consumer Finances tells us that the median home value in 2019 was $225,000. The Freddie Mac House Price Index tells us that the same home in terms of size and location would have cost about $28,500 in 1975.

The 20% starting equity portion for buying a $28,500 home is $5,700. This means the national average homeownership experience was to see $5,700 in home equity at age 25 become $225,000 in home equity by age 69. *The average result for the nation was an almost 40X increase in home equity.* Where did that remarkable increase in wealth actually come from?

The First Level Of Multiplying Wealth

The first level of wealth multiplication is inflation. Based on the Consumer Price Index, the average annual rate of inflation between 1975 and 2019 was 3.6%. Each one of those 44 years and all else being equal, it cost an average of 3.6% to buy most things - including homes - than it did the year before. This means that for each year, we multiplied price levels by 103.6% to get the next year's average prices.

For most people a 3.6% rate of inflation probably doesn't sound all that high, it would be more in the low to moderate range. And indeed one year of 3.6% inflation on starting home equity of $5,700 works out to a $205 annual inflation gain, which is not terribly impressive.

The Second Level Of Multiplying Wealth

However, we didn't have just one year of inflation, but 44 years. This means we had to multiply 103.6% times itself 44 times in a row. This multiplication of the multiplication is the second level of multiplying wealth, and it works with the full power of the compound interest formula. Whether we are looking at investing at a 3.6% interest rate annually or inflation increasing prices at a 3.6% rate, the math is identical, and $100 becomes $475 over 44 years either way.

When we start with $5,700 and multiply it times 475% then we get $27,075. If there were no mortgage - this would be the total new home equity as a result of inflation. And indeed, if we look at any investment that exactly kept up with inflation, whether it be real estate, stocks, gold or silver - what cost $5,700 in 1975 would have a price of $27,075 in 2019, which is an increase of $21,375.

The Third Level Of Multiplying Wealth

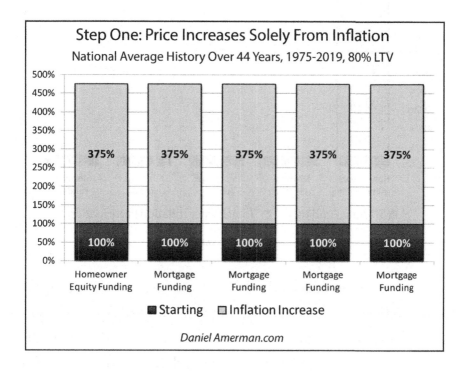

As developed in Book 1, for a homeowner with a mortgage, we stack the 375% inflation gain on top of all five of the buckets, including the 20% starting home equity bucket, and all four of the 20% mortgage funding buckets.

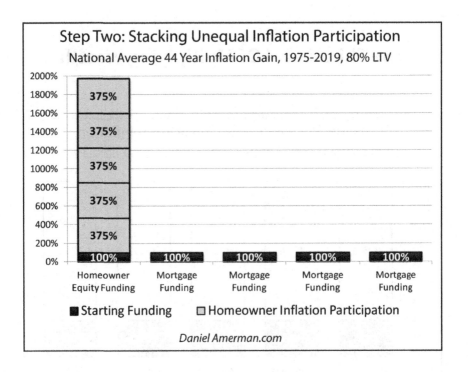

However, because of the unequal partnership, the mortgage lender received none of the inflation gains, and all five went to the home owner. This is the third level of the multiplication of wealth, the multiplication of the compounded inflation gains and the five high stacking to the benefit of the homeowner.

The five high stack is five 375% inflation gains of $21,375 each. What was 100% in starting equity in 1975, becomes 1975% in ending equity in 2019, an increase of almost 20 to 1. (The dual 1975s are an interesting coincidence.)

Considering only inflation and buying the home with a mortgage, the national average was to see $5,700 in home equity at age 25 become $112,575 in equity by age 69.

When we look at this extraordinary increase, then a clear separation emerges between owning a home with a mortgage, versus other inflation hedges. With a normal inflation hedge, an investment that exactly kept up with inflation, $5,700 becomes $27,075. By simply owning a home with a mortgage, with no trading or market timing or brilliant decision making needed, the natural result is to see $5,700 become $112,575, because *inflation is turned into wealth.*

The Fourth Level Of Multiplying Wealth

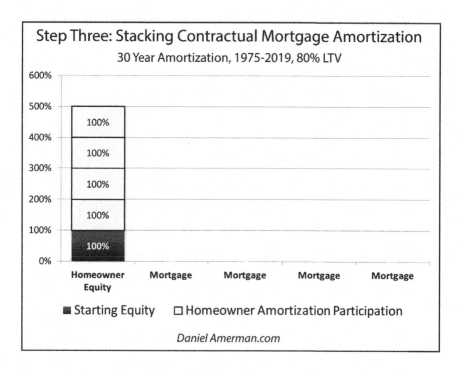

Someone who bought a home at age 25 with a mortgage, and made 30 years of mortgage payments instead of 30 years of rent payments, would have paid off their mortgage by age 55. So by age 69, they would have had 14 crucial years of having a lot more free cash available each month, which could have been very useful for ramping up retirement savings, or just enjoying life, or perhaps helping to put children through college.

What they would have also done is to have taken on the biggest debt in their lives in order to buy the biggest asset in their lives, and then steadily paid down and extinguished that debt over the years, while keeping all the gains from the asset that was initially mostly paid for by the mortgage lender.

Because that mortgage was initially four times larger than the homeowner equity contribution, this is the fourth level of wealth multiplication, which is the multiplication and four high stacking that occurs with amortization increases in equity when a home is purchased with a mortgage

For our average homeowner, their starting equity was $5,700, and four equal sized $5,700 contributions were made by the mortgage lender in order to buy the $28,500 home. All four of the $5,700 debts were paid down over the years through making mortgage payments instead of rent payments. The natural result was to leave the homeowner with the $28,500 home owned free and clear, which is five times the initial equity contribution of $5,700.

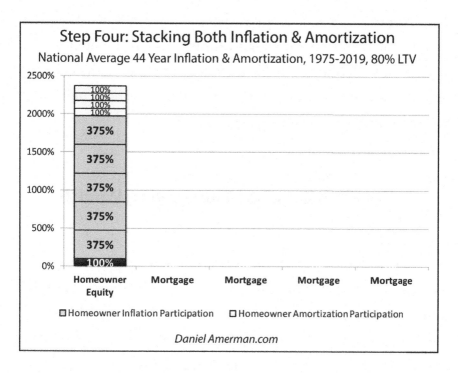

When we combine the multiplications for inflation, compounded inflation, amortization, and the stacking due to the unequal partnership, then we are stacking five 375% compounded inflation gains on top of our initial home equity, and then another four 100% amortization increases on top of that. The combined result of the first four levels of multiplication is 100% in initial equity in 1975 becoming 2375% in equity by 2019, *an almost 24 times increase in equity.*

The completely average and normal outcome for the nation was to have a 25 year old start with $5,700 in savings, and turn that into $135,375 in net worth by age 69, as the natural result of buying a home with a mortgage and thereby benefitting from the first four levels of wealth multiplications.

Not one bit of the extraordinary almost 24 to 1 national average increase is market risk or timing. It is all a matter of alignment with highly reliable government policies, the contract with the mortgage lender, and then multiplying the benefits from the alignment and the mortgage contract.

The Fifth Level Of Multiplying Wealth

The fifth level of the multiplication of wealth is real increases in market value. Once we move to inflation-adjusted terms, removing the compounded multiplication of dollars that is inflation, then a $5,700 housing equity investment in 1975 would have increased by 66% in the year 2019, becoming $9,462. That's nice - but that's it.

For the nation, 44 years of population growth, with more and more of the population living in a more concentrated group of cities with greater density, the increased regulatory burdens associated with building homes in many areas, and the boost from current very low interest rates increasing affordability, all combined with other factors to push the average home prices for equivalent homes up by 66% in inflation-adjusted terms.

If there were no inflation and there was no mortgage, the long term national average is that a 25 year old would have turned $5,700 into $9,462 by age 69, for a gain of $3,762. This is an average gain of about $85 per year.

The Sixth Level Of Multiplying Wealth

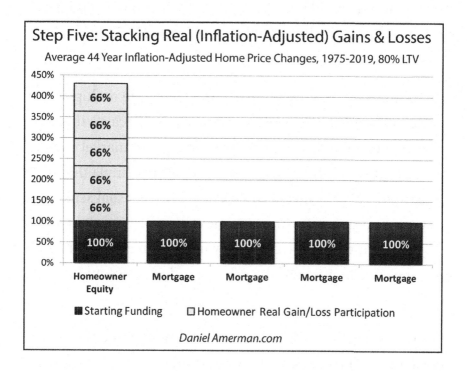

However, for someone who bought a home with a mortgage, then the unequal partnership applies to the real increases in home values, as well as the inflation gains. The homeowner would take all five of the 66% real market value gains from all five of the funding buckets, and stack them all on top of the 100% starting equity, sharing none of the market gains with the mortgage lender.

This is the sixth level of the multiplication of wealth, the multiplication and five high stacking that occurs with real market gains relative to home equity when a home is purchased with a mortgage.

The sum of the five 66% layers is 330%, stacked on top of the starting 100% in equity investment. This means that the equity for the 69 year old would be 430% of what their equity would have been at age 25, as $5,700 would have become $24,510 over 44 years.

In this case, buying a home with a mortgage multiplied the real market value increase in home equity. Because this was borrowing to attempt to benefit from changes in market value, this is the portion of the Homeowner Wealth Formula that is the closest to what is meant by "leverage" in the usual sense. Buy most of an investment with someone else's money, and the price goes up - we multiply the gains. Buy most of an investment with someone else's money and the price goes down - we multiply the losses.

On average over the years, the price of homes did go up in real terms. The five high stacking was then enough to create a more than four times increase in real wealth, even with no inflation.

The Seventh Level Of Multiplying Wealth

When we add four plus four we get eight. When we multiply four times four, we get sixteen - there is an extra eight involved when we multiply two primary sources of wealth, instead of adding them together.

When we multiply inflation gains times real market gains, 375% times 66%, then we get an "extra" 248% in gains. This is the seventh level of the multiplication of wealth, the multiplication of real housing market gains by compounded inflation gains.

For a nationally average 25 year old, the increased financial benefit to them of multiplying a 375% inflation gain by a 66% real price gain, would be to increase their starting $5,700 in equity up to about $19,836 by the time they reached age 69.

Because this seventh level is the result of a multiplication - it is keenly sensitive to changes in either one of the two primary sources of wealth. If there is no inflation or there are no real market gains, then we are just multiplying by 1, and the seventh level of the multiplication of wealth goes to zero.

On the other hand, if there are both significant inflation gains and significant real market gains, then the two primary sources of price gains amplify each other. They also amplify any ongoing changes - so that if real market values go up, inflation amplifies the gains for homeowners, and if inflation goes up, real market value gains amplify the inflation gains.

The Eighth Level Of Multiplying Wealth

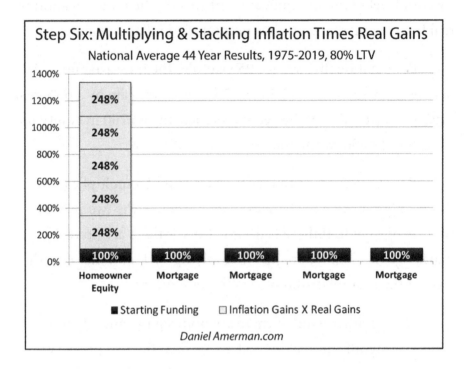

For the next step - let's go back to four plus four versus four times four, but this time let's include a third level of multiplication. Four plus four is eight, *and four times four times five is mind blowing.* Four times four is sixteen, sixteen times five is eighty, and this is ten times the wealth created by adding four and four together.

For homeowners, if starting home equity is one of five buckets, only 20% of the purchase price was put up at closing, and none of the seventh level of wealth creation is shared with the mortgage lender - then we take the multiplication gains from all five of the buckets, and stack them on top of starting home equity.

The seventh level is multiplying 375% inflation gains times 66% real market value gains, to get a bonus level of wealth creation that is equal to 248% of initial home equity. Because this applies to all five buckets, all five of the initial 20% sources of funding, but the gains from all five belong solely to the homeowner, we multiply 248% times five and get 1240%. When we add that on top of the 100% starting equity then *we get an amount equal to 1340% of the starting home equity.*

This is the eighth level of the multiplication of wealth, the multiplication and five high stacking that occurs relative to home equity as the result of the multiplication of real market gains by compounded inflation gains, when a home is purchased with a mortgage.

The secondary increase in wealth that is the mathematically required result of the multiplication of the two primary sources of wealth, inflation gains and real market value gains, is fully stackable - and fully spendable. This is the eighth level of the multiplication of wealth, the multiplication and five high stacking that occurs relative to home equity as the result of the multiplication of real market gains by compounded inflation gains, when a home is purchased with a mortgage.

For a typical 25 year old who put down $5,700 in equity to buy a home in 1975, and experienced the average results for 44 years of homeownership, they would have seen their home equity grow to $76,400 by age 69, just from the 7th and 8th levels of the multiplication of wealth.

(This is the same as the $70,700 number previously developed, when we add back in the $5,700 in starting equity).

Another way of phrasing this is that if we borrow 80% of the money to get the rights to all of the future inflation gains, then we get five times the inflation gains. Similarly, if we borrow 80% of the money to get the rights to all of the future real price gains, then we get five times the real market gains.

However, if we borrow 80% of the money to get the rights to both all the future inflation gains AND all the future real value gains, then the way the math works is that we get a bonus of sorts, a third source of wealth that is not the inflation gains nor the real price gains, but the multiplication of inflation gains times real price gains, that is also then multiplied times five.

Simplified another step, if someone buys a home in a market that is significantly increasing in value at the same time that there is a significant amount of inflation, then they can make a lot more money than can be explained by just the increasing real market values or the inflation by themselves. And if they borrowed most of the money to do that, then the history of homeownership in the United States shows us that this combination of multiplications can create a quite substantial amount of extra wealth, particularly over longer time periods.

As it turns out when we look at national averages over 44 years, the seventh and eighth levels of multiplying wealth are enough to have produced a gain of another 12.4 times starting home equity, over and above the wealth that was already created by the first six levels of the multiplication of wealth.

Comparing The 7th & 8th Levels To Retirement Accounts

Now, this whole concept of multiplying the results of the secondary wealth created by the multiplication of the two primary wealth drivers of inflation gains and real market gains, may, well, sound a bit on the obscure side. Does anyone really need to know these kinds of seemingly odd and complicated technicalities?

Life is an interesting thing, however, and full of many ironies.

We are taught for a lifetime to build wealth through saving and investing, perhaps through passive investment in index funds in a retirement account, but also through much more active means such as learning about stock investment strategies, bonds, precious metals, market timing, trading, option strategies, or perhaps through technical charting strategies.

However, if we look at how our obscure sounding 7th and 8th levels of the multiplication of wealth would have performed for someone who bought a $28,500 home, with an 80% LTV mortgage in 1975 and still owned it in 2019 - about $70,700 of their ending $225,00 home equity would be attributable to those factors. In contrast and as developed in Chapter 1 of Book1, for the about half of the households that do have retirement accounts, the median value of the entire retirement account is less than that, only $65,000.

Indeed, the irony is that for many people in their 60s and 70s, something that they likely didn't even know existed, the stacking of the multiplication of inflation gains times real market gains, may have quietly and gradually made more actual money for them over the decades, than their very intentional long term savings and investments.

To be clear, this is not at all the same thing as saying that those who build wealth through disciplined savings and financial education can't build large portfolios that greatly exceed their home equity. They most certainly can, it has worked out for millions of households, and there can be a life transforming value to the combination of savings, financial planning and financial education. However, in practice, these people are also in the minority, they are not the average person.

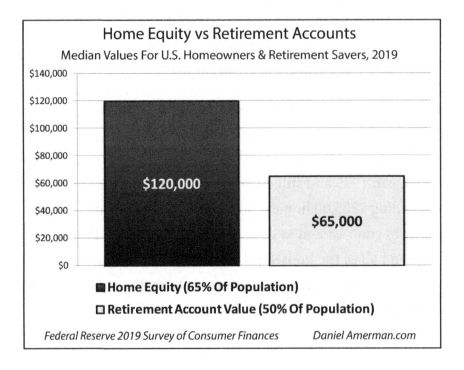

There are fundamental reasons for the discrepancy between home equity and retirement accounts for the truly typical person. What we have just been exploring could be called the combination of three factors, each of which are fundamental, but none of which are intuitive for most people.

The way in which home prices grow with inflation and the power of the compound interest formula is exponential mathematics, which is core to all of mathematics, science and finance – but is not intuitive to the average person. The multiplicative relationship between the compound interest formula and real price gains is not usually intuitive. How the multiplication of the compounded gains is multiplied again when the home is purchased with a mortgage is likely the least intuitive of all.

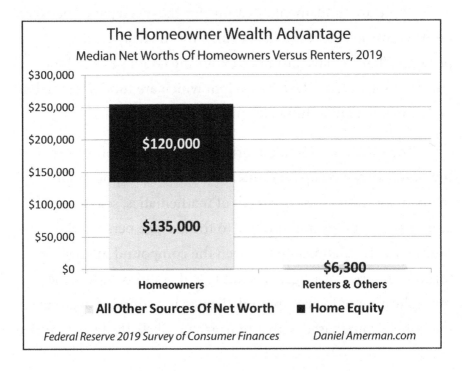

The Homeowner Wealth Advantage
Median Net Worths Of Homeowners Versus Renters, 2019

Homeowners: $120,000 (Home Equity), $135,000 (All Other Sources Of Net Worth)
Renters & Others: $6,300

All Other Sources Of Net Worth ■ Home Equity

Federal Reserve 2019 Survey of Consumer Finances   *Daniel Amerman.com*

But these factors are entirely real. They are the financial fundamentals underlying long term homeownership when the home is purchased with a mortgage. And when these factors are combined, the sheer power of the multiplicative combination becomes so great over a period of decades, *that it should be no surprise that the median net worth for homeowner is indeed a full forty times greater than the median net worth of renters (and others).*

The best time to understand how to deliberately take advantage of those fundamental factors and their multiplication isn't after retirement age - but well before then, and the sooner the better.

Chapter 5

Mapping Out The 19 Sources Of Long Term Homeowner Gains

When we combine all eight levels of the multiplication of wealth, and stack them up on top of the starting homeowner equity, then we get the remarkable stack seen in the graph below.

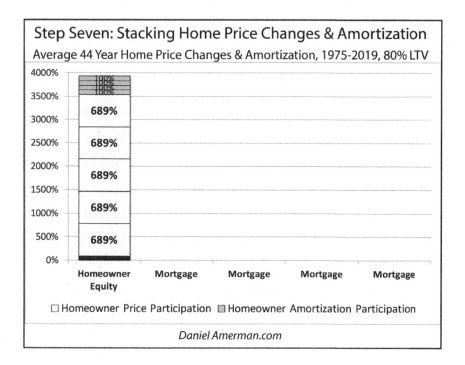

The nationally average homeowner who bought a home in 1975 with 20% down, would have seen their home equity increase by 39.5 times, almost 40 times, by 2019. That is an amazing increase in wealth - and it applies to many millions of households.

The specific prices and years will vary with the household. There may actually be 2-3 or more houses that were owned over the decades, and there were likely some refinancings as well. But the base relationship is a massive multiplication of wealth for those who bought homes in their 20s and 30s, and who were still homeowners but without mortgages in their 60s, 70s or beyond. These extraordinary results are indeed the natural and normal result of long term homeownership.

Dollar for dollar - what were the sources of the largest source of net worth for most households in the United States today?

In this chapter, we will solve that mystery. However, there is an issue – which is that there are 19 sources of the almost forty to one gain. They could not all be displayed in the stacking graph above, as there would have been too many lines and too many numbers. To get them to display, the third level of the multiplication of wealth (inflation), the fifth level of the multiplication of wealth (real gains), and the seventh level of the multiplication of wealth (inflations times real gains) all had to be combined into a single home price increase number of 689%, which was then stacked five high.

A Wealth Map For The Average Homeownership Experience

To better understand the sources of wealth, we will create a map of sorts, and map out each one of the nineteen sources of the forty to one gain.

If someone had bought a home in 1975 using an 80% LTV mortgage, they would have started with a home equity contribution of 20% of $28,500, or $5,700.

We know from the U.S. Bureau Of Labor Statistics and the Consumer Price Index (CPI-U), that on average, what cost $1.00 in 1975 cost $4.75 by 2019.

If we multiply the $5,700 in home equity in 1975 times 375%, then we know that this would increase the number of dollars by $21,375. In other words, we can explain $21,375 of the $219,300 home equity increase just from inflation on home equity, which is 9.8% of the total increase.

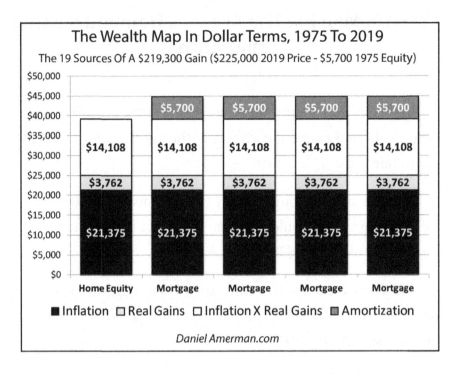

The Wealth Map In Dollar Terms, 1975 To 2019

The 19 Sources Of A $219,300 Gain ($225,000 2019 Price - $5,700 1975 Equity)

This $21,375 increase in home equity can be seen in the lower left bar of the wealth map above, which shows the dollar amounts of each of the 19 sources of the $219,300 national average gain.

That $21,375 is a lot of money relative to the starting $5,700 - but that is the necessary result of compounding an average 3.6% annual rate of inflation for 44 years using the full strength of the compound interest formula.

Another way of phrasing this is that the average homeowner made $21,375 from the first and second levels of the multiplication of wealth, inflation and the compounding of inflation. Crucially, if there is no mortgage - that is all that they would have. A starting equity or investment of $5,700 would have had an inflation gain of $21,375, and that's it.

However, because the homeowner bought the house with an 80% LTV mortgage, they did not just get the benefits from the inflation on their home equity bucket - but all four of the mortgage buckets as well. Inflation gains went solely to the homeowner, not the mortgage lender. The home price of $28,500 included five fundings of $5,700 each, and the $21,375 gains from all four of the other $5,700 fundings went to homeowner equity as well.

This is the third level of the multiplication of wealth - and it is visually obvious that the sum of the five $21,375 gains is the most important source of homeowner net worth by 2019. These five gains, taking the power of compound interest and multiplying times five, total $106,875.

The national average was to earn a six figure gain on an initial $5,700 home equity investment, just from buying a home with a mortgage and keeping all the compounding of the inflation gains over the decades. This primary level of *turning inflation into wealth* with a mortgage explains about 49% of the $219,300 in total homeowner gains.

Paying Off The Mortgage

Another source of increase in home equity is to buy a home with an 80% loan to value mortgage, make mortgage payments instead of rent payments, and steadily pay down the mortgage until the home is owned free and clear.

If there were no inflation and there were no market gains - paying down the mortgage would account for 100% of the increase in homeowner wealth. A $28,500 home is bought with $5,700 down, and $22,800 borrowed. The $22,800 mortgage (four times $5,700) is paid off. The homeowner then owns a $28,500 home free and clear, which is an increase of $22,800 in home equity, and is the fourth level of the multiplication of wealth.

However, in practice as is visually obvious on the wealth map - amortization is not most of the gain, and is indeed a lesser factor. Paying off the $22,800 mortgage only provided about 10.4% of the $219,300 increase in homeowner equity - the other approximately 90% all comes from other sources.

Once this part of the historical wealth map is understood, then it is enough by itself to change many perceptions about mortgages and homeownership. The basic idea is pretty simple. People want to live in a home but can't pay cash, particularly in their younger adult years. They borrow the money to buy the home, and repay the debt on a schedule over many years. Then they own the home with no debt, and can live there without making any more mortgage payments. For many people, this is part of the American Dream, and it also describes their lives.

So, someone who buys a $300,000 home with a $240,000 mortgage will pay off that mortgage over 30 years, and then they would have a $300,000 home with no mortgage. If we go back a few decades, someone buying a $28,500 home would have taken out a $22,800 loan, paid it back over 30 years, and then might have expected to have a $28,500 home with no mortgage.

The increase in wealth that the mortgage opened up, however, was not $22,800 but $219,300. In the past, taking out the mortgage was a key element in opening up gains that totaled about ten times the mortgage amount.

If we look at a more current $240,000 mortgage on a $300,000 home, and if the long term future resembles the long term past, then paying back that mortgage may not open up just a $240,000 increase in net worth, but an eventual $2.4 million increase in net worth over the coming decades.

In other words: 1) Borrow $240,000 to buy a nice place to live a life; 2) pay it back in very small increments over many years; and 3) *end up not with an extra $240,000 in net worth, but an extra $2.4 million.* Most people don't think about it that way when taking out a mortgage to buy a home, but that is exactly how it has historically worked over the long term.

Mapping Real Market Value Gains

After removing inflation related price changes, the national average real value of homes rose by 66% between 1975 and 2019.

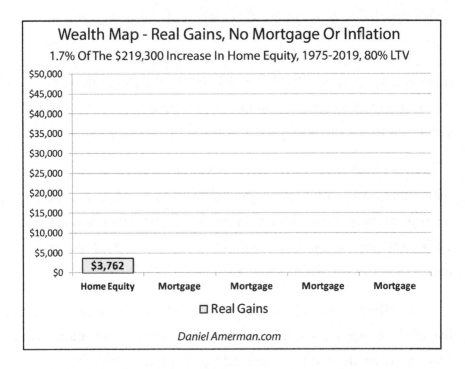

If we isolate that 66% gain on just the $5,700 cash put down, with no mortgage or inflation, then the homeowner would have earned $3,762 over 44 years. That's it, and it is the fifth level of the multiplication of wealth. Real market gains by themselves, with no inflation or mortgage or other multipliers, accounted for only 1.7% of the $219,300 in total home equity gains for the nationally average homeowner.

This is another historically accurate piece of information that is by itself enough to change many common perceptions about homeownership. If asked where that whopping home equity came from after decades of homeownership, many people will talk about their home getting much more valuable and paying off their mortgage. Some may talk about inflation as well, many others may not.

By themselves, in isolation, the combination of the house getting truly more valuable and paying off the mortgage have in practice been relatively minor contributors to long term increases in home equity for the nation. They do not come close to explaining why the median home equity is so high, or why it is such a large percentage of net worth, or why it is almost twice as high as the median retirement account value.

Even with no inflation, buying a home with a mortgage does open up another level of multiplication, the sixth level. The homeowner only put up one funding bucket of $5,700, but they get all the real gains from the four mortgage funding buckets as well. So we put a string of five $3,762 real market gains across the wealth map, for a total of $18,810 in gains for the long term homeowner. With this multiplication, real market gains now account for 8.6% of the total wealth map, the $219,300 increase in home equity.

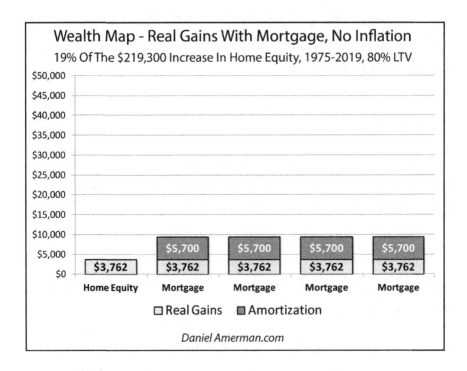

When we combine paying off the mortgage with multiplied real price gains, the fourth, fifth and sixth levels of the multiplication of wealth, then we have all the sources of wealth that do not involve inflation. Visually, while it is respectable, it is only a relatively small part of the surface area of the wealth map.

The total increases in net worth from paying off the mortgage are $22,800, while the total gains from real market value increases are $18,810. Combining those factors accounts for a $41,610 increase in home equity, which is 19% of the $219,300 increase in national average home equity.

This means that the other 81% of the wealth map is all dependent on the existence of inflation, and more importantly - the ability to multiply times inflation.

Indeed, when we look at the wealth map, we can see that the primary historical importance of real price gains over the long term has been their crucial role in unlocking another level of multiplying inflation gains.

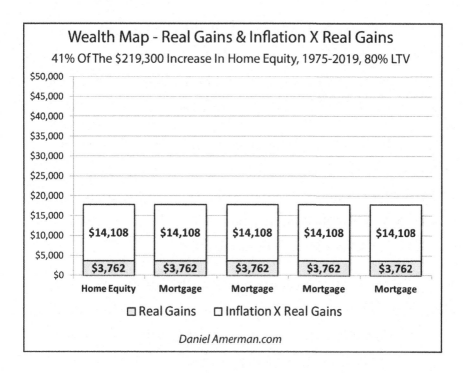

When we multiply the $3,762 real price gain on the starting equity, times 375% in order to account for the 375% more dollars being needed to buy everything, then we get the seventh level of the multiplication of wealth, real price gains times inflation gains, which is equal to $14,108. This one block accounts for 6.4% of the total wealth map, the $219,300 increase in homeowner equity.

Because the homeowner bought the house with an 80% LTV mortgage, we then multiply times five, and put a string of five $14,108 blocks across the wealth map. This is the eighth level of the multiplication of wealth. The sum of those five blocks is $70,538, which accounts for a full 32% of the surface area of the entire wealth map, 32% of the entire $219,300 increase in homeowner equity (this is the same as the $70,700 from Chapter 4, just with different degrees of rounding).

When we stack the home equity blocks on the left, we add the $3,762 real gains block and the $14,108 real gains times inflation gains block, and get a total home equity increase of $17,870, which is 8.1% of the wealth map.

As the house was bought with a mortgage, we then put two strings of five blocks each across the wealth map, a string of $3,762 blocks and a string of $14,108 blocks. In total, the ten blocks add up to $89,348, which is 41% of the wealth map, 41% of the $219,300 total increase in home equity.

If there were no real price gains - the entire 41% in gains that are dependent on real price gains would vanish, and so would almost $90,000 in home equity across the nation, it never would have existed for long time homeowners.

A 24 To 1 Wealth Multiplication - That Is Not Normal Leverage

This brings up an interesting question in solving the mystery of how so much wealth was created for so many millions of people. Are real price gains a critical part of the answer or are they not? On the one hand, real price gains by themselves, with no inflation and no mortgage, account for only 1.7% of the wealth map. On the other hand, when we do include a mortgage and inflation, then with no real price gains, 41% of the surface area of the wealth map would vanish.

Visually, the answer can be seen by comparing one block to ten blocks. Real price gains by themselves are the lower left block of $3,762. However - the other nine blocks in the two strings are all multiples of the single real price gains block. They are therefore completely dependent on the one block, and acutely sensitive to changes in real price gains. Indeed, the top string of four $14,108 blocks on the right are all the multiplication of a multiplication of a multiplication, which means they truly have a hair trigger sensitivity to changes in the first multiplication of real price gains.

When we compare the total gains dependent on real price gains of $89,348, to the single $3,672 real price gains block, then we see that total gains magnify the underlying real gain by 24 times. Every $1 dollar change in the real value of the home - in 1975 dollars - ended up leading to a $24 increase in net worth for long time homeowners in 2019, when measured in 2019 dollars.

Restated, every $1 in gains from the fifth level of the multiplication of wealth became $24 when multiplied times the sixth, seventh and eighth levels.

Now, that 24 to 1 increase is dependent on the actual inflation number, and the 80% LTV mortgage, and is indeed also acutely sensitive to changes in inflation or LTV. However, the core principal remains when it comes to the importance of real price increases for the truly long term creation of homeowner wealth.

Real improvements in the value of the house, whether it be from an improving neighborhood, proximity to the beach, or a lack of buildable land within commuting range, are the "seed" - but they aren't the plant. The plant, and the overwhelming increase in homeowner wealth over a period of decades, are based upon the multiplications, and multiplications of the multiplications, that come with buying the home with a mortgage and then experiencing compounded and cumulative rates of inflation over the many years.

It should also be noted that the 24 to 1 increase is not leverage in the usual sense, but something quite different. The classic "leverage" component is the 5 to 1 multiplication of real gains when 80% of an investment is paid for with someone else's money.

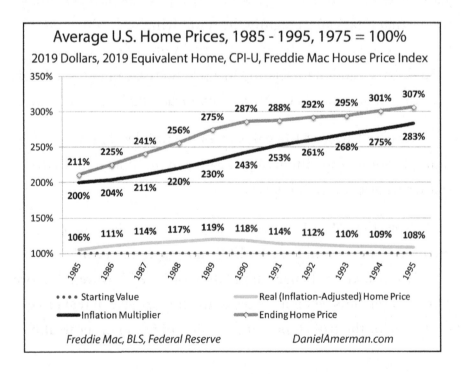

However, as we explored in Chapter 3, and will further develop in Chapter 7, because inflation is a cumulative and one way process as a matter of government policy that grows over time with the power of the compound interest formula - it doesn't just simply multiply the real price gains line in the graph above, but it also changes the slope of the line. Given enough time, inflation generally overpowers real price losses.

With just simple leverage and no inflation, buying a home with a mortgage would have taken the 11% decrease in home prices from the peak of 119% in 1989, and multiplied it times five for five times the losses. However, when we do include inflation, then there is a 32% increase by 1995 from the 275% price in 1989, and it is that home price increase that is then multiplied times five to produce a far larger gain.

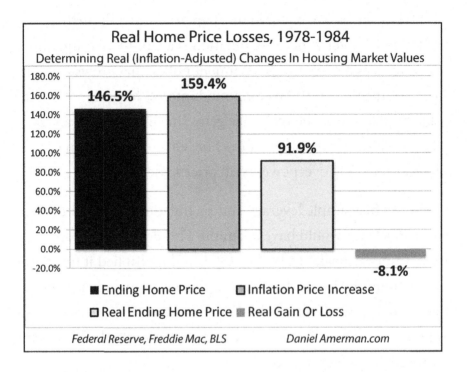

Real Home Price Losses, 1978-1984

Determining Real (Inflation-Adjusted) Changes In Housing Market Values

Federal Reserve, Freddie Mac, BLS   Daniel Amerman.com

Another example is the 8.1% real home price loss between 1978 and 1984 that was explored in Chapter 2. With simple leverage in the usual sense, for a home bought with an 80% LTV mortgage, the 8.1% loss would have been multiplied times five for a 40% loss. However, because inflation completely overpowered the real price loss, there was a 46.5% home price gain, that when multiplied times five, became a 232% gain in just six years. A major loss was transformed into a quick and huge gain (even in inflation-adjusted terms).

Over the long term, by changing the slope of the price line from negative to positive, the Inflation Multiplier also completely transforms the usual leverage formula - making all outcomes positive.

The range of outcomes then becomes not amplified gains versus amplified losses, but rather amplified gains versus lesser but still substantial gains. When real home prices are rising, and real price gains and inflation are working together as a multiplicative team, then the outcomes can be amazingly good, such as the historical 24 to 1 multiplication of the underlying gains that was the average homeowner experience over those years. However, when real home prices are falling, the ability of inflation to overcome those losses (given time) still sets up a multiplied and major gain, just not as large as the gain would be with rising real home prices.

This is a very unusual and highly advantageous relationship that works strongly to the benefit of homeowners (and investors), it is a dominant feature of the wealth map for how wealth has been created for a nation in practice, and it is simply not there with other traditional investment categories.

Chapter 6

Rapid Wealth Creation From Nineteen Sources

In the previous chapter we looked at the 19 sources of total homeowner wealth creation over the very long term. The astonishing almost 40 to 1 national average increase in home equity was driven primarily by giving inflation and the exponential power of the compound interest formula almost half a century to run, and then turning that inflation into wealth with further levels of multiplication.

Those numbers are not as large when we look at shorter time periods. Nonetheless, history shows us that even at much lower power levels, the nineteen sources of gains in home equity are still enough to very rapidly create wealth, with potentially life changing results in the first 3 to 10 years.

As determined by the Federal Reserve's *2019 Survey Of Consumer Finances*, for those who own their primary residences, their median home equity is equal to almost half of their total net worth, meaning it is by far their largest investment. The graph below shows total increases in that largest component of net worth by years of ownership, from the time they bought their home with an 80% LTV mortgage.

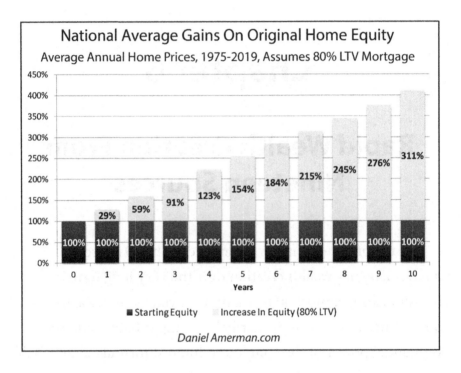

There were 42 possible three year homeownership periods between 1975 and 2019. The nationally average outcome for homeowners over those decades was to see their home equity increase by 91%. So, there is no need to wait for anything like retirement age to reap the benefits of the Homeowner Wealth Formula.

Indeed, a 30 year old buying in any year between 1975 and 2016, would have on average seen their home equity almost double by age 33. This near doubling of the likely largest component of net worth for that 30 year old in just three years could have had life changing implications - *and it is the national average.*

The national average homeownership experience for homeowners was to see a 215% increase in their home equity in seven years. A 30 year old who bought a home in any year between 1975 and 2012, would have on average experienced a tripling in their home equity - which was likely by far their largest source of net worth - by age 37.

For ten years of homeownership, the national average experience was for home equity to increase by 311%. On average, history shows us that a 30 year old buying a home in any year between 1975 and 2009 would have quadrupled their home equity by age 40.

These are extraordinary, life changing increases in net worth and financial security, and they are just the national averages. To better understand where these remarkable results for the homeowners of the nation came from, we can break out wealth maps of the 19 sources of homeowner gains for the near doubling, the tripling and the quadrupling.

Almost Doubling Home Equity In Three Years

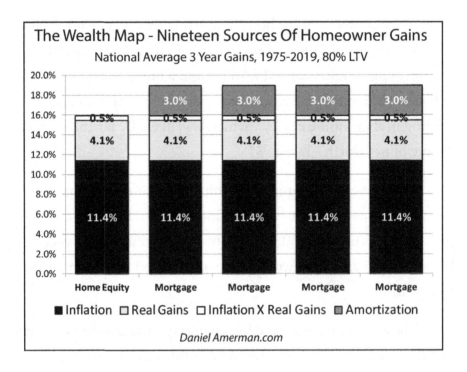

When we move to much shorter time periods - then most of the gains from the compound interest formula disappear. Looking at all 42 of the possible three year homeownership periods, on average, prices for most things rose by 11.4% over three years. Almost all of this was the first level of the multiplication of wealth, the multiplication of home prices by three annual rates of inflation. Very little was the second layer of the multiplication of wealth, the additional gains from the multiplication together of those annual rates, as the needed time for the compound interest formula to work its magic just wasn't there.

When we move to the third level of the multiplication of wealth, and put a string of five inflation blocks across the map as a result of the unequal partnership and the homeowner keeping the inflation gains from all five buckets of funding, then even low rates of inflation with very little compounding are still enough to visually dominate the wealth map.

Indeed, when we combine the five inflation blocks together, they add up to a 57% price gain, which accounts for 63% of the total 91% increase in home equity over three years, or almost two thirds of the total.

On average over the decades, only 3% of the starting mortgage balance was paid down in the first three years of homeownership. However, as explored in Chapter 8 of Book 1, when we take into account that there are four mortgage funding buckets for every one home equity bucket, we get the fourth level of the multiplication of wealth, and a string of four 3% amortization blocks across the wealth map. The four 3% amortizations combine to increase home equity by 12%. So even though paying off 3% of the mortgage seems very small, it was nonetheless enough to drive about 13%, or one eighth of the 91% total three year increase in home equity.

Once we adjust for inflation, the national average real increase in market values for homes was 4.1% in the first three years, and this is the fifth level of the multiplication of wealth. The 4.1% is the entire gain if there is no mortgage, and there is either no inflation, or we adjust for inflation. It accounts for only 4.5% of the 91% total increase in home equity.

When the home was purchased with a mortgage, however, and the homeowner keeps the real market value gains from all five of the funding buckets to themselves, sharing none with the mortgage lender, then we get the sixth level of the multiplication of wealth, and put a string of five 4.1% real market gains across the wealth map. The total of 20.5% for the five real market gains accounts for about 22.5%, or almost a quarter, of the 91% total increase in home equity.

As covered in the previous three chapters, the seventh level of the multiplication of wealth, multiplying real gains times inflation gains, is acutely sensitive to changes in real gains, as well as to changes in inflation gains. When we move to the far smaller average inflation gains and real market gains associated with three years of homeownership - this secondary source of wealth creation almost completely collapses down to a mere 0.5%. When there are big numbers to multiply together, the seventh level becomes very important, with small numbers for either inflation or real market gains - it almost disappears.

It is still there, however, and that means there is a string of five across the wealth map, as the result of the eighth level of the multiplication of wealth. In total, the five 0.5% blocks add up to 2.5%, which means that they account for 2.7% of the 91% total increase in home equity.

All of the numbers for the sources of wealth become much, much smaller when we move from 44 years of homeownership down to 3 years. But, there are still 19 of them, 19 sources of increases in home equity when a home is purchased with an 80% LTV mortgage. And when we add all 19 up - we get something extraordinary.

The average homeownership experience has been to almost double home equity in the first three years. If someone has $40,000 in starting home equity, and that is most of their net worth, their average experience was to have that grow to $76,000 in just three years.

That is an enormous leap in net worth in a very short time - how else does somebody do that?

What kind of risks would they have to take with most of their net worth to almost double it in three years?

How lucky would they have to be?

Yet, that is the typical and normal homeownership experience, the natural flow of wealth for a nation over the decades.

This also raises an interesting counterpoint when it comes to the dilemma of coming up with the cash to pay for the equity for a first home. For good reason, the amount of money is large enough that it is difficult for some people to picture how they could do that. It just may not be convenient for what their vision is at that time in their life of where they want to live and how they to live.

The counterpoint is - what else could a younger person possibly do that could on average nearly double their net worth in three years? Once that bridge of buying that first home is crossed, whatever is involved in getting there, then a life changing path for rapid wealth gains has historically naturally opened up for the new homeowners that is simply unavailable for renters. The earlier those gains are opened up, then the greater the benefit over a lifetime.

Tripling Home Equity In Seven Years

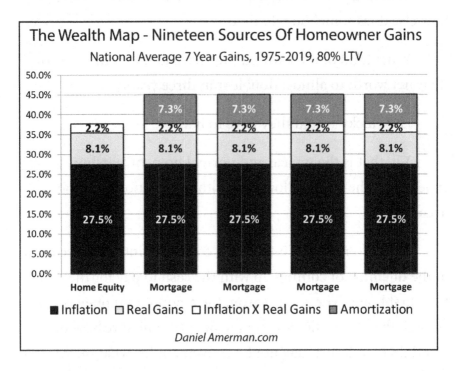

When we move to the national average homeownership experience over the first seven years of homeownership, including all 38 of the possibilities between 1975 and 2019, then the numbers get much better.

We are now putting a string of five 27.5% blocks of inflation across the wealth map for a total of 137.5%. In other words, inflation by itself more than doubles starting home equity over seven years, when a home is purchased with a mortgage.

When we give mortgage amortization another four years to work, then the national average has been to pay off 7.3% of the mortgage over seven years. Because the mortgage is much larger than home equity, but all the benefits flow through to home equity, a string of four amortization blocks is created, and this is enough to increase home equity by 29.2%, which is becoming significant.

Real market value gains in seven years averaged about 8.1%. Buy the home with a mortgage, put a string of five real market value gains across the wealth map, and the average has been a 40.5% increase in homeowner equity as the result of the house becoming genuinely more valuable over seven years.

The seventh and eighth levels of the multiplication of wealth remain small, but they are the product of the multiplication of both larger inflation gains and larger real market gains. There is therefore a disproportionate increase in wealth when both of the primary wealth drivers of wealth are increased. This secondary creation of wealth increases by 4.4 times, 0.5% to 2.2%, giving a little hint of what it can do. When five blocks are strung across the wealth map, the total is an 11% increase in home equity. To put it in perspective, this little understood factor is now up to about 38% of the importance of the much better known factor of paying down the mortgage.

Once again, there is an array of 19 sources of increases in homeowner equity, with the best known sources being the real value of the home increasing by 8.1%, while the mortgage was paid down by 7.3%. Even the largest block of a 27.5% increase in price levels over seven years as a result of inflation is not that large, this is still low to moderate inflation.

But nonetheless, for someone who buys a home with a mortgage, and enjoys living in a nice place for seven years while making mortgage payments instead of rent payments, the average changes in home equity and net worth are astonishing.

The norm over the decades for many millions of households has been to a little more than triple their home equity in their first seven years of homeownership. Some seven year periods were better, some were worse, but the average was to see $40,000 in home equity become $126,000 in home equity. That is a life changing difference in net worth for most families - and it is the typical outcome.

How else does a typical family get that result as an average outcome?

(Or a typical investor?)

Quadrupling Home Equity In Ten Years

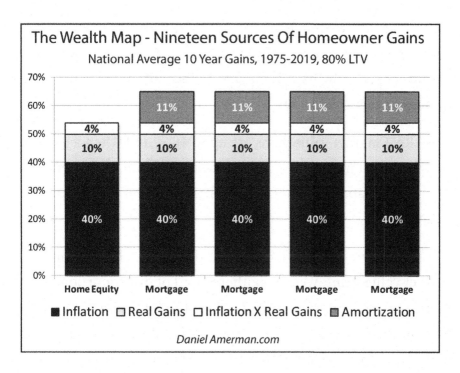

When we go out ten years, and average the results from all 35 of the ten year homeownership periods between 1975 and 2019, then we get the wealth map above. The numbers - and the wealth creation - are rapidly getting larger as each of the fundamental wealth drivers have more time to work, with the results then being multiplied across the map for all them together.

The total gain from inflation is now up to 40%, and the compounding of inflation is starting to matter, although not as much as it will be in another decade or two. When we string the five inflation gains across the wealth map, we get a 200% increase - a tripling of home equity, just from inflation and buying a home with a mortgage. Another way of phrasing this is that by ten years, the inflation string by itself is nearly as important as all 19 sources put together on the seven year wealth map.

On average over the years, 11% of the mortgage would have been paid down, and when we put the four part string across the wealth map, this by itself is enough to increase homeowner equity by a very respectable 44%.

Real market value gains are up to 10%, and when a home is bought with a mortgage and five blocks are strung together across the wealth map, then real gains by themselves increase home equity by 50%.

When we multiply larger inflation gains by larger real market value gains, we get another round of disproportionate increase in secondary wealth creation. The total after ten years is now up to 4% - which is almost twice what it was at seven years, and 8 times what it was at three years. When strung across the map, this secondary creation of wealth is now enough to increase home equity by 20%.

By ten years, the national average for many millions of households was that a crucial stage had been reached. If we just take mortgage amortization, real market gains and secondary wealth creation, then they add up to 114%. By themselves, they are enough to more than double homeowner equity in ten years. That is a very good outcome, and while there are other ways of doing it, this is difficult to match as an average outcome in ten years.

At the same time, and on a different part of the wealth map, inflation and multiplying inflation is enough to triple homeowner equity in ten years. That is much harder than doubling wealth, and it is truly difficult to find alternatives that can triple wealth in ten years as an average outcome.

As time passed, and all eight levels of the multiplication had time to build strength, history shows us that wealth creation was being driven by two very powerful groups of multiplications.

Buy a house with a mortgage, and the multiplications of real market value gains and mortgage amortization are almost enough to double homeowner equity in ten years by themselves, and they are more than enough when we include the multiplication of the secondary wealth gains.

Separately, buy a house with a mortgage, and inflation and the multiplication of inflation gains are enough by themselves to triple homeowner equity.

Those are two powerful groups of sources, each individually remarkable, that when combined were enough to more than quadruple starting home equity. The national average outcome over ten years was to take $40,000 in home equity and turn it into $164,400 in home equity.

That is an amazing number for just ten years. How else can an average person do that? But yet, on a percentage basis, that 311% increase in home equity is the historically normal outcome for buying a home with a mortgage, and then experiencing ten years of nationally average results for all 19 of the sources of home equity gains.

(Sharp-eyed and mathematically oriented readers may be wondering if some of the numbers are a little bit off. For instance, real market gains averaged 4.1% when looking at the 42 three year homeownership periods, but only 10% when looking at the average of the 35 ten year homeownership periods. Shouldn't the total ten year gain be closer to 14%?

The explanation is that the data base includes only periods for which we have the actual historical data. As of the 2019 data, which was the last full year available while this book was being written - we didn't know the ten year price gains for a home purchased in 2010, let alone 2013 or 2016. On the other hand, we did have good three year price gain data for all home purchases between 2010 and 2016. Those were, on average, very good years for real price gains for housing. The shorter the time period of homeownership - the heavier the weight for the generally strong housing market of the 2010s. For one year of homeownership, 9 of the 44 possibilities were home purchases between 2010 and 2018, so 20% of the weight for average outcomes comes from the 2010s. For ten years of homeownership, none of the 35 possibilities start in the 2010s, so there is a zero percent weight.

The same factors are in play when it comes to inflation and amortization.)

Chapter 7

Falling Real Home Prices & Using The Formula To Reduce Risk By 80%

As reviewed in previous chapters, when we look at the average outcomes, then real home price changes that are not the result of inflation are a strongly positive force. On average over the decades, these market based price changes add around 1% per year to the benefits of multiplied inflation and amortization. Because real home price changes are themselves multiplied, along with their associated inflation, this has historically been enough to raise the increase in national average home equity from 3.4 times starting equity without real values changes, to 4.1 times starting equity with real market value changes.

However, when we look not at the average of outcomes but the full range of outcomes - then not all homeowners experienced positive outcomes for real market value changes. Indeed, there were quite a substantial number of losses over the years.

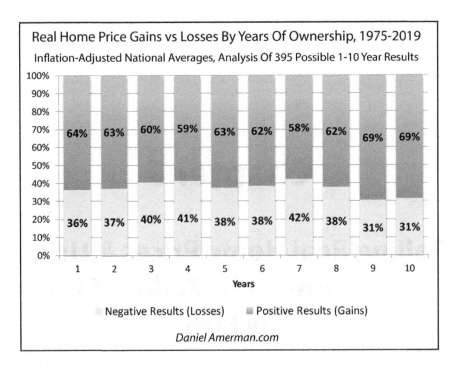

Out of the 395 possible 1 to 10 year homeownership periods - housing lost value in inflation-adjusted terms 148 times. The chance of a loss peaks at 42% for seven year homeownership periods, and is the lowest at 31% for nine and ten year homeownership periods. In total, the national average homeownership experience has been to lose money on the price of the home in inflation-adjusted terms about 37% of the time.

Now, that sounds bad - but this is a really tough test, and there are very few investments or assets that are available to the average person that can consistently pass it. If we look at stocks in inflation-adjusted terms, then most of the long term profits disappear and the chances of losing money in stocks over 1-10 years goes way up. Even if we look at a traditional inflation hedge like gold, once we adjust for the purchasing power of the dollar - gold loses value in inflation-adjusted terms close to half of the time, and can do so for decades.

Losing money on the value of the cash in your pocket or in the bank happens every year as a matter of national policy. If we look at money in the bank, particularly since 2008, then you are likely receiving close to a zero percent interest rate - as a matter of government policy. Meanwhile as a separate (but related) matter of policy, the government does its best to reduce the value of the dollar every year. The two policies of near zero percent interest rates and somewhat higher rates of inflation come together like a pair of scissors - and the average saver loses money in inflation-adjusted terms 100% of the time, as a matter of government policy.

What real estate, stocks and gold have in common is that they are all considered to be inflation hedges, where the number of dollars needed to buy those assets increases even as the number of dollars needed to buy everything else also increases. In their own quite different ways, real estate prices, stock indexes and gold prices all compound upwards over time with the compound interest that is inflation. For the average family home to be able to do that - and exceed it - most of the time is a remarkable achievement, when placed in perspective, and this by itself places homeownership in a more sophisticated and rarified investment territory than most people realize.

The Worst Of The Worst

When we look not at averages but at the worst of the worst - the worst cases out of all the possibilities - then we get a quite different picture than what we saw with the averages.

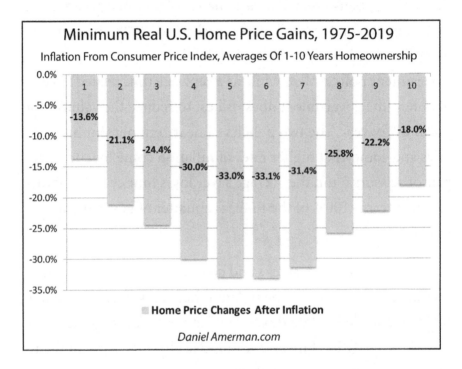

The graph above shows the absolute worst results for real changes in market value out of all 395 of the 1 to 10 year homeownership periods.

Out of the 44 one year possibilities, the worst outcome was 2007-2008 when the average American home lost 13.6% of its value on an inflation-adjusted basis.

If we go out to three years, then the worst case experienced by the average homeowner out of 42 possibilities was to see the real market value of their home go down by 24.4%, and this occurred in the years 2006-2009.

The worst of the worst, out of all 395 possibilities was the six year decline in national average inflation-adjusted home prices of 33.1% that happened in the years 2006 to 2012. Looking at annual averages on an inflation-adjusted basis, 2006 was the peak of the real estate bubble, and 2012 was the very bottom of the collapse of the real estate bubble, so those six years being the worst of the worst is exactly what we would expect.

Things get better past six years, but even if we go out to ten years the worst outcome of the 35 possibilities was to have a real market value loss of 18%, and this happened in the 2005 to 2015 period.

What do all of those worst outcomes out of all of the possibilities have in common? They all consist of buying at the worst possible time for homeownership, close to the absolute peak of the real estate bubble. To actually get the full loss, they then need to sell at the worst possible time, out of all the possibilities for a home bought in that year. Indeed, every worst case loss involved selling right into the teeth of the worst financial crisis in generations, the Financial Crisis of 2008 and its aftermath. Call it "Murphy's Law" times two, for the truly unlucky - buy at peak home prices and then sell into an economic and financial disaster.

The Multiplication Of The Worst

There is a particular problem with losses when it comes to buying an asset primarily using other people's money, in this case buying a home while using a mortgage lender's money to pay for 80% of the purchase price. Because of the unequal partnership, we get all the gains and we multiply the gains times five. However, the catch is that if there is a loss, then because of the unequal partnership, we get all the losses for all five buckets, and we have to multiply the losses times five.

That is what leverage is all about - multiply the gains if we get it right or are lucky, multiple the losses if we get it wrong or are unlucky. Many fortunes have been made using leverage - and many fortunes have been lost using leverage.

As explored in Book 1, what separates the Homeowner Wealth Formula from ordinary leverage is that it is mostly based on inflation and amortization, i.e. governmental policy and a contractual relationship. Because this is the case, we don't see the large market swings associated with ordinary leverage, but instead see 100% positive outcomes for the combination of inflation by itself, and amortization.

However, when we remove inflation, ignore amortization, and isolate real changes in market value in the purchasing power of the price of the home - then we do get numerous losses, and some are quite large. Compounding the difficulty is that when we find the worst of the worst, we need to take those losses and multiply them times five to determine the impact on homeowner equity.

If we look at the worst case of losing 13.6% of the real value of a home during 2007-2008, the worst possible timing, then we need to take that 13.6% loss and multiply times five, for a 68% loss in homeowner equity.

Using the example of a $200,000 home bought with $40,000 in equity, each bucket would lose 13.6%, which is $5,440. However, the mortgage is not reduced for the real market value losses with the four $40,000 mortgage buckets, and we still owe the same amount of money. So, we take the hit from all five buckets in homeowner equity which is five times $5,440, and that is a total of a $27,200 loss. Starting with $40,000 in beginning equity, that would leave us with $12,800 in remaining equity, which is indeed a loss of 68% of our equity.

The very worst of the worst was buying in 2006 in the very peak year, feeling the full force of the Financial Crisis of 2008, and then selling in 2012 at the lowest of the (inflation-adjusted) post-crisis home prices. That ultimate "Murphy's Law" combination (at least for national averages) produced a maximum loss of 33.1% - which then needs to be multiplied times five because of the unequal partnership.

Take a 33.1% loss in real market value, multiply times five, and the unfortunate homeowner would take a 165.5% loss on their home equity. They would lose 100% of their beginning equity, and then another 65.5% (relative to their beginning equity), because of their mortgage now being larger than the real market value of their home.

For a $200,000 home bought with $40,000 in equity, the five buckets would each take a 33.1% hit , which is equal to $13,240 each. Because of the unequal partnership, the sum of all five of the losses, which is $66,200, would be taken by the homeowner. This would wipe out their starting $40,000, and leave them with a $160,000 mortgage, and a home that was worth $133,800, meaning that they would be "underwater" by $26,200. The homeowner would owe $26,200 more on the home than its real (inflation-adjusted) market value.

It is the worst of the worst if we isolate the most volatile component of real home price changes and then multiply it - but it isn't what actually happened, or at least not to the extent that the average homeowner could tell that it happened. Because in practice, there was inflation. In practice, there was mortgage amortization. In combination, on a national average basis, inflation and amortization have been much more powerful than real changes in market value.

Overpowering 72% Of Market Losses With Inflation

Real market losses can be a powerful force for homeowners losing value. But history shows that there is a much more powerful source of losing value for savers and a nation, and that is the unstoppable, cumulative, one way force of inflation.

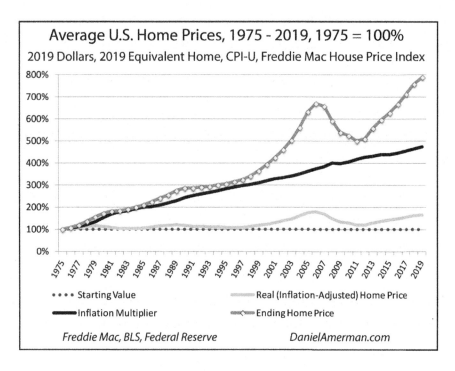

Keep in mind that inflation is expressed by it taking more dollars to buy almost everything each year, with a base low to moderate rate of inflation being a matter of governmental policy (in the form of the Federal Reserve). Yes, each individual dollar buys less - but this is expressed by it taking ever more dollars to buy things like homes, as shown with the steady upward slope of the Inflation Multiplier line.

As an example, let's take a look at an unusually bad, long term and substantial market decline in the real value of the average American home that was not associated with the real estate bubble or the Financial Crisis of 2008. The national average U.S. home lost 9.7% of its real market value, the purchasing power of the dollars that it could be sold for, between 1989 and 1996. Multiplied times five, that would have cost the homeowner almost half of their home equity over seven years - and real estate investors half their equity as well - if it weren't for inflation.

Remember that awful time when an entire nation lost almost half of its home equity? It is highly unlikely that any readers do, because almost no one realized that it was happening at all, even as it happened.

Inflation between 1989 and 1996 meant that it took about 27% more dollars to buy most things in 1996 than it had in 1989. This was not a particularly high rate of inflation, but was in fact almost exactly average. When we look at all 38 possible seven year homeownership periods between 1975 and 2019, the average is a 27.5% increase in the number of dollars it took to pay for an average standard of living.

Crucially, real market losses are not an actual negative number - but rather a reduction from 100%. To get the dollar impact of a 27% gain, we add 100% to 27%, and we then multiply the value of the house times 127%. As explored in Chapter 2, to get the dollar impact of a 9.7% loss, we subtract 9.7% from 100%, and multiply the value of the home times 90.3%.

We start with a home value of 100%, and reduce it to a real value of 90.3%, because that was an unusually bad period for the housing market. However, we then need to multiply times 127% - because that is what inflation is, taking more dollars to buy the same things. The 127% is the Inflation Multiplier line. The product of that multiplication, 127% X 90.3%, is 114.3%, so including inflation left us ahead about 14%. If we are just looking at this the way almost everyone usually looks at things, the average homeowner saw a 14.3% increase in their price of their home between 1989 and 1996.

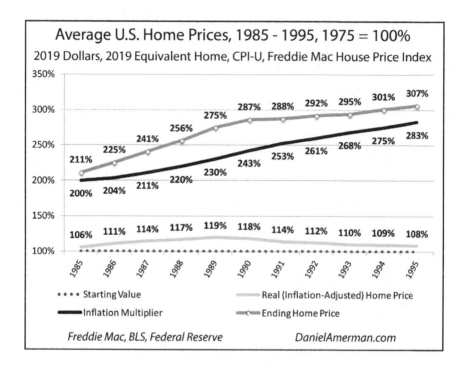

Average U.S. Home Prices, 1985 - 1995, 1975 = 100%
2019 Dollars, 2019 Equivalent Home, CPI-U, Freddie Mac House Price Index

Freddie Mac, BLS, Federal Reserve   DanielAmerman.com

We can see the same relationship for every year from 1990 to 1995 in the graph above that was developed in Chapter 3. Every year, the Real Home Prices line fell, the Inflation Multiplier line climbed, and the product of their multiplication rose as can be seen by the slope of the Ending Home Price line. This is the usual outcome for negative changes in real market value. Inflation usually more than offsets the real market value loss, and the price of the home usually rises - just not enough to keep up with inflation.

We then need to take that multiplied result, and multiply it again, for the 80% LTV mortgage and the five high stacking for 1989 to 1996. For the nationally average homeowner this meant that their home equity increased by a little over 70% in seven years - during one of the worst periods for homeownership (in terms of the real value of homes) before the Financial Crisis. That's why homeowners don't remember this "awful" time - because they turned even a moderate rate of inflation into so much wealth that it was not only able to overcome the real market losses, but to create a quite attractive increase in their home equity.

This should have been a battle between two behemoths, a particularly severe real decline in home values versus a moderate rate of inflation. In practice - it was no contest. The compound interest formula in the form of inflation has been such a powerful and reliable flow of wealth over the years, that it overwhelms most real market losses, without the homeowner ever realizing their home price was ever doing anything but going up, up and up.

When we look at the "battles" between real losses in market value for the 395 possible 1 to 10 years homeownership periods between 1975 and 2019, then there were 148 instances of losses in real, inflation-adjusted home prices on a national average basis. However, once inflation is taken into account, and we are just looking at simple dollars with no inflation adjustment - then there are only 42 instances of home price losses.

One way of phrasing this is to say that including inflation removes 106 out of the 148 real market losses, meaning that inflation reduces the risk of falling home prices by 72%.

Another way of looking at it is that because only 42 out of the 395 possibilities are negative when we include both real home market value changes and inflation, then what history has shown is an 89% chance of a positive increase in home prices. With every one of those 89% of the outcomes that are positive then being multiplied times five. Let me suggest that having an almost 90% chance of getting to multiply a positive outcome times five is some pretty remarkable odds, odds that are very difficult to find with any other form of investment (let alone gambling).

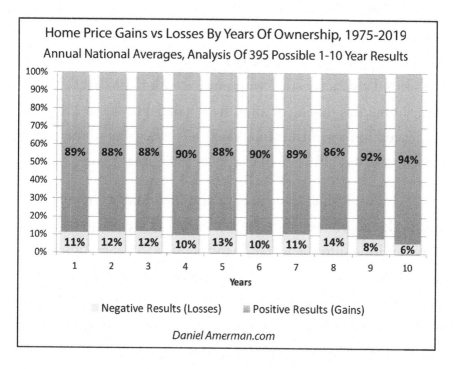

This relationship can be seen for each year of homeownership in the preceding graph. For the 1975 to 2019 era, there was an 89% chance that the price of a home would go up in the first year it was owned, and an 11% chance it would fall in value. Looking out six years, the national average home increased in price 90% of the time, and it fell in price 10% of the time.

Going out a full ten years, there was a 94% chance of an increase in price, and a 6% chance of a decrease.

This brings up a really interesting question - given the sheer power of inflation: what does it take to lose money? How is it even possible that a homeowner could lose money 11% of the time?

As it turns out, when individually looking at each of the 42 instances of falling home prices, they shared two uncommon characteristics. The first is that the purchase of the home occurred between 2003 and 2010, in the time when the housing market was dominated by the growth and collapse of the real estate bubble. The second characteristic - with one exception - is that the sale of the home was during or after the Financial Crisis of 2008. The only exception was that immediately after the peak of the bubble, home prices did fall 1.5% in the 2006-2007 time span.

So, it took an extraordinary combination of 1) buying in a market dominated by a bubble in real estate prices, and then 2) selling into the worst financial crisis in generations to generate a loss in total home price. There were eighty 1 to 10 year homeownership periods that started between 2003 and 2010, and 38 of those did not result in losses, so even in that period, almost half of the homeowners did not experience losses on a national average basis.

What gets even more interesting is when we leave the period of the real estate bubble. Of the 395 one to ten year homeownership periods between 1975 and 2019, 315 of them started before 2003, or after 2011. Out of those 315 possibilities, the number of losses experienced by homeowners on a national average basis for any 1 to 10 year homeownership period was - zero.

Looking at the nation as a whole and away from the bubble and the crisis, there were 87 times that homes lost market value in real terms. And in all 87 instances, inflation more than covered over the loss, and in fact generated a total gain instead of a loss.

Homes have market risk - of course they do! Like anything else, supply goes up and down, and there are good markets and bad markets. But inflation doesn't go back and forth, it is instead a steady, crushing one way destruction of the value of the dollar as a matter of government policy. This inflation is expressed by it taking an ever increasing flood of dollars to buy things, driven by the power of the compound interest equation in a relentless and cumulative process.

When we take that ever increasing flood of dollars - it is, as we have reviewed, far more important on average than market risk changes in home prices. And indeed what history shows us is that inflation has been so powerful and so reliable relative to true market price changes in home values, that it has been 100% effective in generating positive home price gains for homeowners when we get away from the combination of the housing bubble and the financial crisis of 2008.

That has been the average national experience - out of the 315 possibilities that were not part of the bubble or crisis, there were 315 gains looking at total prices, which means there was 100% effectiveness in generating gains. And then for homes purchased with an 80% LTV mortgage - there was also 100% effectiveness in taking those gains and multiplying them times five. The reliability and power of this natural flow of wealth has been astonishing for U.S. homeowners.

To be clear - these are national averages, which are the best measure of the homeownership experience and the flow of wealth for the nation as a whole. In practice, there is a lot of variation when we move away from national averages - individual metro areas can move differently, individual neighborhoods can move differently, and individual home prices can change in ways that are quite different than national averages. So some people did lose money during those years, of course they did and likely quite a bit of money in some cases, but their experience was not the norm, and for every person experiencing below average results, there was someone else experiencing above average results.

Using Inflation Plus Amortization To Reduce Risks By 80%

The national average homeownership experience grows even stronger when we include mortgage amortization, and stacking those increases in home equity four high.

When we include both amortization and inflation, then the number of times that homeowners experience losses falls from 148 losses in real market value, to only 31 decreases in actual homeowner equity, out of the 395 possibilities.

This means that inflation and amortization were enough in practice to overpower real market value losses a full 80% of the time. They couldn't do it all of the time, inflation and amortization were not enough to overcome that double Murphy's Law situation of a historic real estate bubble and a deep crisis that nearly took down the global financial system - but outside of those cases, inflation and amortization were 100% effective in preventing losses on a national basis.

Even with the bubble and crisis, if we include amortization, then the chances for a homeowner seeing their home equity increase rises to 92%, over all 395 of the one to ten year possibilities.

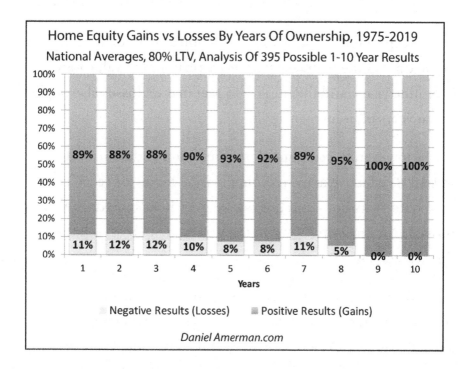

Also of importance, as can be seen in the graph above - this increase is not even. All of the chances for losses disappear for nine and ten year homeownership periods, even taking the worst of the collapse of the bubble and financial crisis into account.

Inflation is a one way process over time as a matter of policy. Amortization is a one way process over time as a matter of contract. The farther out that we go in time, the more powerful that inflation and amortization each become, the more powerful still that the combination becomes, and the greater its ability to overcome real market losses.

Time is very forgiving for homeownership and market risks, because of inflation and amortization. The longer that someone just lives in their home, the more insulated from market risks they become, and the greater their ability to turn inflation into wealth.

Keep in mind that without inflation and amortization, 31% of the time homeowners experienced real market value losses over nine years, and the same 31% real market losses also applies to ten years of homeownership.

However, the combination of inflation and amortization was 100% effective at overcoming market losses, once we go at least nine years out - and this is true even if we include the worst possible timing with regard to the real estate bubble and the financial crisis.

To see how this worked, let's return to our worst possible (national average) case for ten years of homeownership. That particularly unlucky homeowner would have bought in 2005 at almost the top of the real estate bubble, and then taken the full blow of the Financial Crisis of 2008. By 2015, the real market value of their home would have still been down by 18%. Because they purchased the home with an 80% LTV mortgage, that loss needs to be multiplied times five. So, just looking at real market value, this particularly unfortunate homeowner should have been sitting on a 90% loss of their beginning home equity, ten years out.

There is yet another element of Murphy's Law in play here. For it wasn't just the real estate bubble and the financial crisis that were the problems, but this occurred during a time of particularly low inflation. How many more things could go wrong for that poor homeowner?

Remember, inflation can be a homeowner's best friend over time, and the historic average is for the price of everything - including homes - to rise from 100% to 140% over the course of ten years. That 40% increase would have easily overwhelmed the 18% real market loss, and generated a nice gain to then multiply times five.

However, this particular unfortunate homeowner would have only benefited from about half the normal rate of inflation, with price levels in 2015 being only 21.4% higher than they were in 2005. Multiplying a real home price in 2015 that was only 82% of what it was in 2005, times it taking 121% times as much money to buy things in 2015, and the combination was that the home price was still down by 0.25%, or a quarter of one percent. That loss would be multiplied times five, so the homeowner would be down by 1.25% on their home equity.

Before amortization, that is. About 16.6% of the mortgage would have been paid down, as the homeowner finally caught a break. (This is a result of the relationship between inflation, mortgage rates and amortization speeds, as explored in Chapter 8 of Book 1.) This would increase their home equity to 33% (in comparison to their starting 20%), which is a gain of 64% over ten years.

Even in this worst case scenario with enormously bad luck hitting from three directions - buying at the near peak of a historic bubble, getting hit by an enormous financial crisis, and then experiencing particularly low rates of inflation - the combined power of inflation and amortization was still enough to flip what should have been a 90% loss in real market value, into a positive 64% gain in homeowner equity.

There was a 100% success rate with time, inflation, and amortization overcoming real market losses for homes owned at least nine years. There was a 100% success rate for time, inflation and amortization overcoming real market losses for homes owned at least one year on a national average basis, so long as they were not purchased in the years 2004 to 2010.

Those 100% success rate numbers are fairly amazing, but there is no getting around that homes have market value risk, even on a national average basis. So do stocks, bonds and gold, among many other types of investments and assets.

What is different about homeownership is that most of that risk - 80% of it historically - has been removed by the primary sources of the increases in homeowner equity, which are inflation and amortization. What is left has been substantially reduced, with inflation and amortization working to reduce the degree of losses.

Risk Reduction From Inflation & Amortization

The risk that remains is also reduced by the combination of inflation and amortization. If we look at the worst of the worst out of the 395 possibilities for real losses, the 2006 to 2012 period when national average real market value losses were 33.1%, there was a 13.9% increase in price levels and there was also 8% of mortgage amortization over the six years. Take the 113.9% of the money needed to buy everything, multiply it times 66.9% of the remaining real market value, and the price of the home fell by 23.8% in actual dollars. We then have five blocks of 23.8% losses because of the mortgage, but we also have four blocks of 8% increases in equity because of the amortization of the mortgage.

When we put it all back together the loss in equity was about 87%, so there was still 13% remaining in home equity, and the home was not "underwater" in terms of owing more on the mortgage than what the market value of the home was. Inflation and amortization combined to cut the loss almost in half, compared to the 165% loss in home equity that would be the result of just taking the 33.1% real market value loss and multiplying times five because of the mortgage.

With the passage of another 3 years, the combination of a recovering housing market along with further inflation and amortization were enough to get the homeowner "back in the black", with a national average home price and home equity in 2015 that were higher than they were at the time of purchase in 2006.

If inflation had not been so low - then the results could have been quite different. If inflation had increased price levels by 45% over the six years, then the combination of inflation and amortization would have produced an actual home equity increase even with the "worst of the worst" real price change.

Indeed, with anything over a 49.5% inflationary increase in price levels over six years, the home price itself would have risen, because when we multiply 149.5% times the 66.9% remaining real market value, we get 100%, and no price loss. (The inverse property of multiplication means that 100/66.9 X 66.9/100 = 1, 100/66.9 = 149.5%, 149.5% X 66.9% = 100%).

This ability of inflation to overwhelm even steep real market losses over time is very useful information to keep in mind for people who are concerned that the 2020s and 2030s may bring higher rates of inflation at some point.

Chapter 8

Getting Lucky & The 23% Chance Of Getting The Price Of A House For Free

In the previous chapter we examined the consequences of being unlucky - owning a home during the 37% of the time that there were real market losses. Inflation in combination with amortization was able to overcome that adversity about 80% of time, leaving the homeowner with a positive increase in home equity.

When we moved out to at least nine years of homeownership, or away from the bubble and crisis, then there were positive results 100% of the time on a national average basis. Some of them were pretty small, but at least they were positive, and home equity did increase.

What happens if we get lucky instead of unlucky?

What history shows us is that there is about a 23% chance over ten years that lucky homeowners will experience an increase in home equity that is about equal to what they paid for their home in the first place.

Rounded to the nearest whole number, in 8 out of the 35 one to ten year homeownership periods between 1975 and 2019, homeowners on a national average basis saw their home equity increase by an amount equal to five (or six) times their beginning equity. Multiplying a 20% beginning equity times five, they gained about 100% on top of that. In other words, the homeowners of the nation got the equivalent of about what they paid for the home, as a bonus, on top of the beginning equity that they also still had.

This effectively getting the price of a home for free sounds improbable, something that is too good to be true. But yet, this 5 times increase over and above starting equity, this equivalent of getting the original price of a house for free, is indeed what historically happened almost one quarter of the time. (They still have an amortized mortgage at that point, so not 100% equity at the new home price in 10 years, but their equity did go up by an amount about equal to the *original* full home price.)

If they bought a $200,000 dollar home with 20% down - the lucky homeowners gained about another $200,000 over the next ten years. If they bought a $400,000 home with 20% beginning equity - then about 23% of the time the fortunate homeowners on a national average basis gained somewhere around another $400,000 in home equity over the next ten years.

This could be thought of as effectively getting a lottery ticket with each mortgage payment. If the homeowner with an 80% LTV mortgage gets lucky, then when ten years are up, they get the equivalent of the entire original purchase price of their home as a lottery prize.

What makes this even better, however, is that there are actually two "lotteries", and two types of "lottery tickets". Historically, there are there are two different primary sources of the five times gains, and either one is enough to win the home equity lottery.

Maximum Real Home Value Increases

As explored in Book 1, homeowners have successfully turned inflation into wealth 99.7% of the time, if we look at the usual impact of inflation in isolation. Increases in real market value have been a powerful source of new wealth over the decades, creating positive wealth gains 63% of the time.

What this means is that almost two thirds of the time all eight levels of the multiplication of wealth have been simultaneously working in favor of the homeowner.

As developed in the last chapter, the inflation and amortization levels of multiplication have historically been able to "overpower" the real market loss levels about 80% of the time, still delivering positive home equity gains for the homeowner. There is, however, a price – which is that much of the gains are used up in flipping the total home equity change to positive. That is much better than taking a loss, but history shows that the mixed homeownership periods, where some levels of the multiplication of wealth are working against each other, are not where the best returns occurred.

The maximum gains are always the result of having all eight levels of the multiplication of wealth being positive and working together. To see how powerful this combination can be, we will begin by looking not at the minimums, but the maximum real market value gains for homes on a national basis. Just how strong have they been?

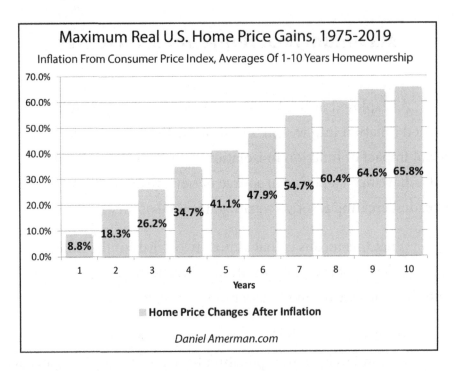

Stripping out inflation, the maximum real (inflation-adjusted) gain in home values over three years was 26.2%, and that occurred in the 2002 to 2005 period. Now, one could say that this was just the inflation of the bubble and the homeowners just gave it all back when the bubble popped - but that isn't true. For homeowners who got in early in the bubble, they never did give it back and all ten of the 1 to 10 year homeownership periods starting in the year 2002 produced positive results.

There was an almost 50% gain in real market value in the six years from 1999 to 2005. While that would go down in the financial crisis, this gain in real market value was so powerful in combination with inflation, that even if we look at the ten year 1999 to 2009 period, into the very depths of the Great Recession - the national average homeowner still saw their home equity increase to become 3.9 times greater than where it started. So, homeowners who bought in 1999 made money hand over fist as the real estate bubble inflated, and built so much equity via the Homeowner Wealth Formula, that they were still far ahead even after the bubble collapse and the crisis. People don't talk about that much, but it is history, it is the experience of a nation, and it is crucial.

The absolute peak for ten years was the 65.8% real market gain between 1996 and 2006. While these analyses stop at ten years, this gain was so large in combination with inflation and amortization, that homeowners who bought in 1996 came through the bubble collapse and Great Recession with a tremendous amount of home equity intact, and then started building equity again with the next rebound in the housing market.

What the worst cases for real home gains and the best cases for real home gains have in common is that they are each associated with the real estate bubble - but they aren't the same years at all. The maximum losses came from buying very late, very close to the top. The maximum gains came from buying early - and those gains were so strong that they were persistent, and were not wiped out by either the collapse of the bubble or the crisis.

Multiplying Two Sources Of Gains

In Chapter 7 we looked at the worst of the worst, and out of all 395 of the one to ten year homeownership periods that have been experienced by the nation, if someone was really, truly unlucky – what happened?

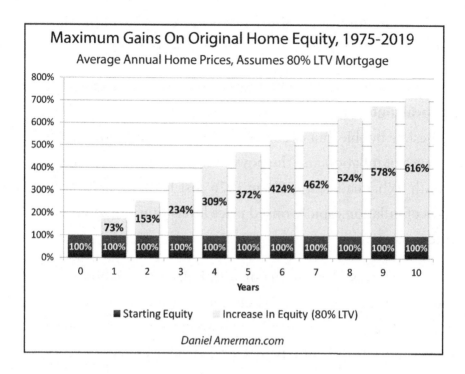

The graph above examines the opposing question - what happened when the homeowners of the nation got lucky?

What all ten of the historical maximum wealth creation outcomes for the nation had in common is that all eight levels of the multiplication of wealth were positive.

Inflation was positive, as it was 99.7% of the time as a matter of governmental policy.

Real market changes were positive, as they were 63% of the time.

Mortgage amortization was positive, as it was 100% of the time as a matter of contract.

The multiplication times five occurred 100% of the time with an 80% LTV mortgage, as a matter of contract.

To see how this wealth was created, let's take a look at the peak outcome for 3 years. This was not associated with the real estate bubble, but occurred during the years 1976 to 1979, because of inflation and the power of turning inflation into wealth. What had cost 100% in 1976 cost 127% by 1979, as high rates of inflation rapidly raised price levels - including home prices.

There was a second major wealth driver - real home market values rose by 13.8% between 1976 and 1979. And the combination of inflation and real market values is multiplicative. So we multiply inflation by real market value increases, 127% times 114%, and total housing prices for the nation on average rose to 145% of where they started.

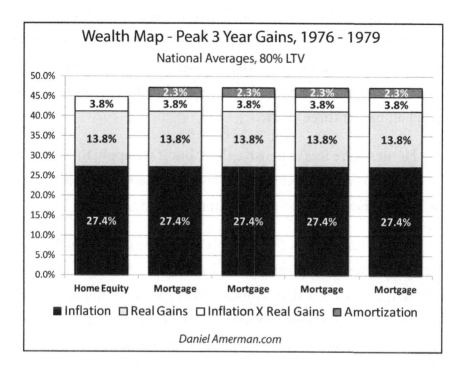

We put a string of five 27.4% inflation blocks across the wealth map because the home was bought with a mortgage, for a total of 137%. Inflation by itself, when turned into wealth via a mortgage, was enough to more than double homeowner equity in just three years.

We also put a string of five real market gains of 13.8% across the map for a total gain of 69%. With both inflation and real price gains being significant, their multiplication is a respectable 3.8%, and there were total gains of 19% from the five blocks. Amortization was minimal over three years, but the four 2.3% blocks were still enough to increase home equity by another 9%.

As we saw in Chapter 6, the average of all 42 of the three year homeownership periods was a still remarkable 91% gain, almost doubling home equity. The 1976 - 1979 period was the best of the group, the top out of all 42 possibilities, and in this case homeowner equity more than tripled in three years. The total increase in home equity from the 19 sources on the wealth map was 234%, meaning home equity increased to 3.3 times of what it started at, in just three years.

Homes were less expensive then, but if we apply those percentages to more modern price levels, $40,000 in home equity would have increased to $133,600 in three years.

That is amazing, but what is even more important is the specifics of when it happened. The value of the dollar fell by 21% in those three years. The inflation-adjusted value of the Standard & Poor's 500 stock index also fell by 21%. A recession had just ended in 1975, and another was about to begin in 1980.

And right in the heart of this time of financial turmoil, high inflation and battered stock markets (a combination some fear we could see again) - is the exact time that the Homeowner Wealth Formula delivered its maximum three year benefits to the nation, increasing home equity by 3.3 times right when the homeowners needed it the most - as a natural flow of wealth. Or at least, there was a natural flow to the homeowners (and income property investors), for the renters it was just a matter of seeing their rent soar upwards while the purchasing power of any money they had in the bank or in the stock market was plunging.

Peak Wealth From Eight Levels Of Multiplication Over Six Years

Now 3.3 times the money in just three years is very good - but the farther out in time we go, then the more powerful that the combination of the two primary wealth drivers of inflation and real market value increases becomes, as do all of the 19 sources.

The peak wealth creation for the homeowners of the nation over six years was to see their average home equity increase to being about five and a quarter times higher than where they started, and this occurred between 1975 and 1981.

In this case, relatively high annual inflation rates and giving the compound interest formula six years to multiply the dollars needed to buy most things - including homes - increased prices to 169% of where they started. Real home market values also rose by 7% over the six years.

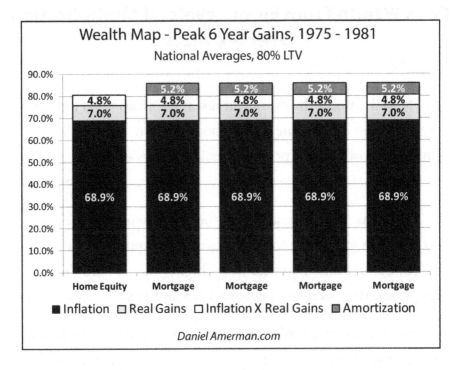

The overwhelming dominance of inflation and turning inflation into wealth for peak six year gains is visually obvious in the wealth map. The inflation blocks are a towering 69% each, and when we string them across the map because the home was bought with a mortgage, the total gain is 345%, which accounts for about 81% of the surface area of the entire wealth map.

The 7% real market value gain was quite respectable, just a little over the long term average for six years, and the total for the five blocks was a 35% increase in home equity.

Because inflation was high and real market gains were respectable, the secondary wealth creation from the multiplication of the two primary drivers was almost 5%, and totaled 24% from all five blocks.

Because amortization had more time to work, a little more than 5% of the mortgage was paid down, and that was then multiplied times four. Combining all the elements of the increases in home equity, on a national average basis, the homeowners of America increased their home equity by 5.24 times over six years.

For a $200,000 home, equity would increase from $40,000 to about $210,000 in just six years, which was a gain of about $170,000. Now, this isn't quite yet gaining the original home price of $200,000 that was referenced in the chapter introduction - but it took place in only six years, not ten years.

What makes this average experience for the homeowners of the nation even more impressive is the six years in question. By extending to 1975 and 1981 - the six years now include at least parts of three different recessions. The dollar fell by 41% in purchasing power. The S&P 500 stock index fell by 12% in purchasing power. These were really bad years for the economy and for the value of money in the bank, but the Homeowner Wealth Formula stepped up again, multiplied both wealth drivers, naturally turned them into wealth, and delivered 5.24 times the money, right when it was needed the most.

As for the renters?

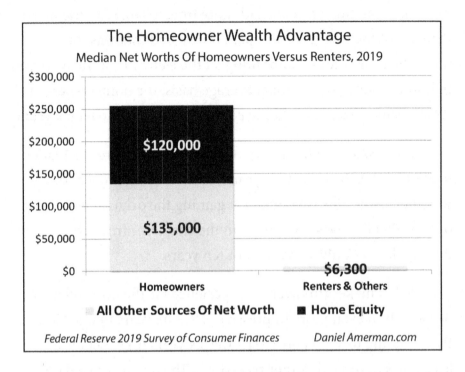

The years 1975 to 1981 are a particularly strong example of the forces that help to create the 40 to 1 median net worth advantage for homeowners over renters, even many decades later.

The first half is the top part of the stacked bar, the home equity that surged by more than five times in six years. That is an extraordinary gain that was reserved exclusively for homeowners. Renters did not participate (although the owners of the rental properties did, which is important information for investors who are concerned about inflation today).

Of at least equal importance is that to the extent rents increased with inflation - a renter would have been paying 70% more in monthly rent in 1981 than they did in 1975. And they had to hope that their income rose by 70% as well, otherwise they could have faced crippling financial pain in trying to make the far higher rent payments.

A homeowner would have been making the same monthly principal and interest payments in 1981 as they were in 1975. If their income didn't go up by 70% because of inflation - they would still be fine. And if their income did go up by 70% - then mortgage payments would be much smaller as a percentage of their income, and that then freed up A LOT of their monthly cash flow.

That is what actually happened in the 1970s and 1980s in particular and it has continued through this day, although in not quite as powerful of form. That freed up monthly cash flow has in practice bought a lot of investments over the years - increasing the net worth in the bottom half of the stacked bar - as well as paying for many vacations and quite a few college tuitions.

The monthly cash flow benefits for homeowners over time is the subject of Book 3 in this series. In practice these increases in monthly free cash flow have been every bit as powerful and financially beneficial for homeowners with mortgages over the years as have the increases in home equity that are the subject of Books 1 & 2.

Maximum Wealth Creation From The Eight Levels

The single largest gain in real market values for homes occurred between 1996 and 2006 when the national average home rose in value by about 66% over ten years. What this represented was a perfect capture of all of the gains from the entire real estate bubble, and none of the losses (that began in 2007).

Inflation is the dominant source of the increases in home equity for the maximums for all the one to six year homeownership periods, with all of those occurring in the 1970s and 1980s. When we look at the maximum gains for seven to ten year homeownership periods, the dominant source of gains moves to increases in real market values, and these were for periods ending in 2005 or 2006, at or near the peak.

An increase of about 66% over ten years is impressive - but if that is all that there is to it, then home equity had only increased to 1.7 times of where it started. Many people look at real estate and homes as being a matter of trying to anticipate real changes in market value and making a smart investment. With no inflation and no mortgage, the payoff for perfection - the brilliant choice to buy in 1996 and be in a home for ten years - the single best outcome out of all 395 possibilities, was enough to multiply the money the homeowner put down to buy the house by 1.7 times.

In other words, $40,000 would have become $66,400, which is gain of $26,400. That's not bad, but for a brilliant market timing move - the single best ten year investment period - it isn't all that impressive either.

However, what has created so much wealth for so many millions of American homeowners over the decades wasn't perfect market timing, but rather having eight levels of the multiplication of wealth, with all eight of them pulling together in the same direction.

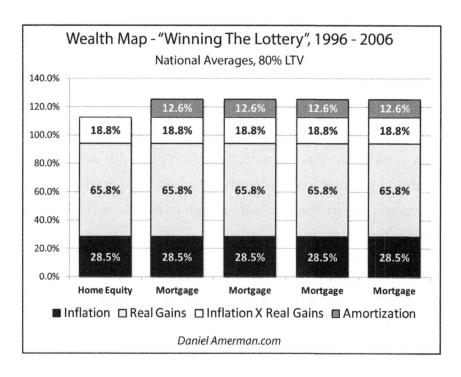

When we break out the wealth map, we have a new visually obvious dominant source for the increases in home equity. Because the home was bought in the best possible year, we have a 66% national average real gains block. Because it was bought with a mortgage, there is a string of five 66% blocks across the map, for a total of a 329% gain. This is most of the wealth map - but all fourteen of the other sources of home equity gains are also of significant size.

The inflation block of 28.5% becomes 142.5% when all five blocks are included. So, when we look at homeowner gains and maximum wealth creation, inflation was increasing homeowner wealth by close to 150%, even while real gains were contributing about 330%.

Because both real gains and inflation gains were substantial, the secondary wealth creation from their multiplication is a quite substantial 18.8%. When that seventh level of the multiplication of wealth is then strung across the wealth map as the eighth level of the multiplication of wealth, the total increase in home equity is 94%. Just this secondary creation of wealth from having two strong primary wealth drivers for a home purchased with a mortgage, was by itself almost enough to double homeowner equity in ten years.

The average mortgage in 1996, based on the 7.80% average rate for that year, would have paid down by 12.6% by 2006. Take the amortization based increases in home equity, string four of them across the wealth map, and that is another 50.4% increase in home equity.

When we take all 19 sources of increases in home equity, ranging from 12.6% up to 65.8%, we get a total increase in home equity of 616%. This means that out of all 395 possibilities, the single best result for the nation was for the average homeowner to have 7.2 times the equity that they started with. That is an amazing number for being a national average over just ten years, and for just being the natural result of being a homeowner with a mortgage.

If someone had purchased a $200,000 home with $40,000 in equity in 1996, and had just experienced the national average increase in home prices by 2006 - they would have ended with a total equity of $286,400, which would represent a $246,400 increase in home equity. That gain was equal to 123% of the entire $200,000 original purchase price of their home - the homeowners of the nation did indeed collectively win a lottery of sorts, with the prize being a gain that was larger than the starting price of their homes.

It is also worth noting that even in this maximum period for real market value gains, the 66% real gain component is only about 11% of the 616% total increase in home equity. The other almost 90% of maximum wealth creation was all in the inflation and the mortgage, and the multiplications of the multiplications.

The Resilience Of Having Two Sources Of Maximum Wealth Creation

When it comes to the importance of having two distinct primary sources of home price increases, inflation and real market value, it isn't just the crucial multiplication of the two that matters. There is also a diversification that occurs, in that either source can take the lead when it comes to multiplying home equity.

The source of maximum homeowner wealth gains can be a powerful bout of inflation multiplied times even moderate increases in market value. It can be a powerful surge in real market values for the nation, multiplied times even moderate inflation. Either way, from either source, there is a quick and powerful natural flow of wealth to homeowners with mortgages.

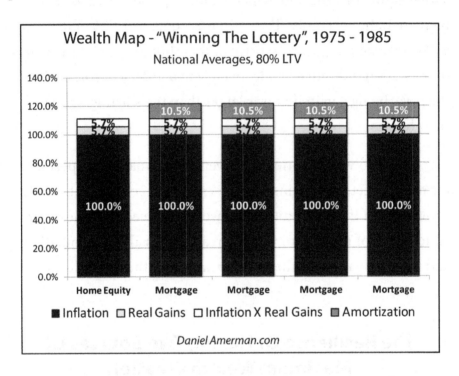

While the peak ten year home equity wealth gain of 616% from 1996 to 2006 was primarily based on real market gains supported by inflation, it is visually obvious on the wealth map above that the second most powerful wealth multiplication came primarily from the other primary source, that of inflation.

Between 1975 and 1985 the number of dollars needed to buy most things rose by 100%. When we string five 100% blocks across the wealth map, we get a 500% increase in home equity.

Because a 5X gain on the 20% initial equity is equal to the original purchase price of the home when the home was bought with a mortgage - inflation by itself was able to produce a gain equal to the purchase price of the home in ten years. This also qualifies as "winning the lottery", although it was done with the inflation lottery ticket rather than the real market value ticket.

The other 14 sources of increases in home equity were much smaller - but they added up. A 5.7% real price gain still added up to 28.5% when strung across the wealth map. Because real gains were smaller, so was the secondary creation of wealth, but it added a total of another 28.5%. Mortgage amortization over ten years was 10.5%, and that was another 42% gain from four blocks.

In sum, the rest of the sources provided another 99% in home equity increases. They were enough to almost double home equity by themselves, on top of the five times increase from the primary effects of inflation, for a total of a 599% gain. This can also be expressed as the national average homeowner having about seven times the home equity they started with, with $40,000 in initial home equity becoming $279,600.

The seven times increase in wealth is accurate in terms of how the world usually looks at price changes. However, it is useful to take a closer look at inflation when so much of the gain is produced by inflation. If there were no mortgage and we adjust for inflation, then the total gain is the single real gains block on the left side of a 5.7% gain. Both the primary and secondary wealth gains from inflation of 100% and 5.7% would disappear, and there would be no amortization. If there were $40,000 in initial equity, it would become $42,280 over the ten years.

The difference between a $2,280 gain and a $239,600 gain is inflation, the mortgage, and turning inflation into wealth with a mortgage. When we adjust for inflation by dividing the total new home equity by 2 - as it took $2 in 1985 to buy what $1 would have in 1975 - we still get a 3.5X increase in home equity. That is a still massive increase in equity in a time of turmoil, and it is almost entirely the result of stringing the inflation gains across the wealth map, as well as the real gains and the real gains times the inflation gains.

Still More Lottery Wins

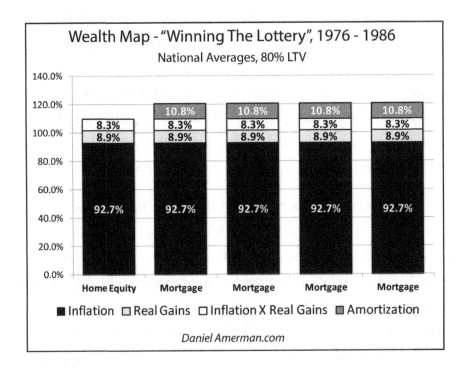

The third lottery win was from 1976 to 1986, and it was another win for the inflation lottery ticket. Inflation was a bit lower with five 92.7% blocks strung across the wealth map, however real gains were a good bit higher, with five 8.9% blocks. Having more real gains to work with boosted the secondary wealth creation of inflation times real gains to 8.3%, which were also then strung across the map. Amortization was also just a bit higher, with four blocks of 10.8%.

The national average total gain for homeowners in those years was 592%, and of that, the five inflation blocks provided about a 463% gain, and the other 14 sources in combination were enough to provide a 129% gain, more than doubling home equity by themselves.

For a $200,000 home bought with $40,000 in initial home equity, home equity would have risen to $276,800. This $236,800 increase in home equity in ten years would have again exceeded the original entire home purchase price, and across the nation, the many millions of homeowners who bought in 1976 did indeed on average "win the lottery" by 1986.

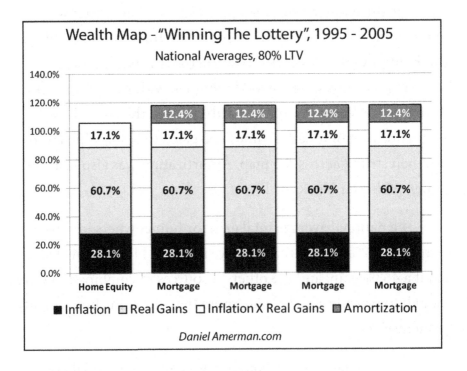

It was the real market value ticket that drove the fourth lottery win, for homeowners who purchased in the year 1995. By 2005 real market values had increased by 60.7%, and when strung across the wealth map, produced a total gain of about 303%. Real gains by themselves were enough to quadruple home equity, when the house was purchased with a mortgage.

However, the other 14 sources were all significant as well, with 28.1% inflation, 17.1% secondary wealth creation from multiplying real gains times inflation, and 12.4% mortgage amortization. When multiplied and strung across the wealth map, these sources produced a combined 276% gain - meaning they were almost enough to quadruple home equity as well.

When we add all the gains together, then the total national average gain was 579%, which was an increase in equity to about

6.8X of where it started. For a $200,000 home, $40,000 in starting equity would have become $271,600, for a $231,600 gain that exceeded the original home price, and the many millions of homeowners who bought in 1995 did on average "win the lottery" as well.

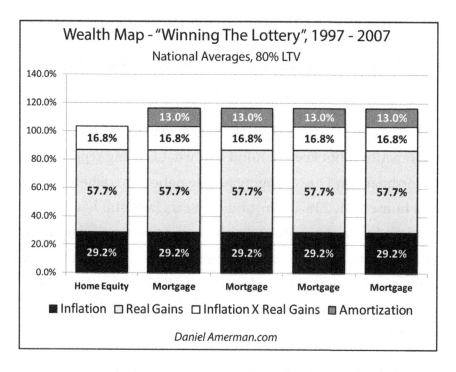

The real market value ticket also drove the fifth lottery win, for people who bought a home in 1997. Real housing market values rose 57.7% by the year 2007, and produced a total gain in home equity of about 288%. The other 14 sources were all significant as well, producing a total gain of about 282%. For those who bought in 1997, they experienced a very balanced and substantial increase in wealth, with the amount being produced by the primary driver of real market gains being almost exactly equaled by the other 14 sources of home equity increases.

Total gains were 570%, which is an increase to 6.7X the starting home equity. Starting with $40,000 in equity, the average experience was to see that become $268,000 in home equity. This gain of $228,000 in ten years exceeded the $200,000 original home price, for yet another lottery win.

A Repetitive Success Story For The Nation

My apologies to the reader if this is starting to sound a little repetitive, but keep in mind that what is being repeated is extraordinary and life changing for the nation as a whole. To buy a house with 20% down, and ten years later still have that equity, and then the original purchase price on top of that sounds somewhat fantastic, or even wildly improbable. How many people go into a gas station to buy a lottery ticket, or into a casino to play the slots, and then walk out with a $200,000, $300,000 or $400,000 win?

To win that kind of money playing the lottery or the slots is a pure fantasy scenario for most people. A lot of people will try, but very few will succeed. However, with homeownership - it was the completely normal and average national outcome. Millions of people bought homes in 1975, as they did in each of the years of 1976, 1995, 1996 and 1997. They didn't know they were buying lottery tickets, they thought they were just buying a nice place to live. And because most people don't have the money to pay cash for a home, most of those millions of home buyers in each of those years took out mortgages as well.

But nonetheless, intentional or not, the national average homeownership experience for the entire nation in each one of those years for those who bought with an 80% LTV mortgage, was to indeed effectively "win the lottery". (As was also true for the real estate investors who bought expecting more moderate returns and got lucky instead.)

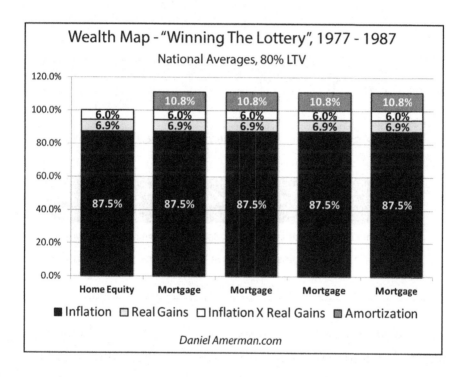

There was another lottery win for the millions who bought homes in 1977, with the advantage shifting back to the inflation lottery ticket. The primary wealth driver was an 87.5% inflationary increase in price levels, which when multiplied times five becomes a 437% increase in home equity. The other 14 sources of home equity increases were lesser, but in combination added up to a 108% increase, and were therefore enough to double homeowner equity on their own.

The total gain was 545%, which is an increase to almost 6.5X the starting home equity over ten years. Starting equity of $40,000 would become $258,000, a $218,000 gain that exceeded the $200,000 original price of the home.

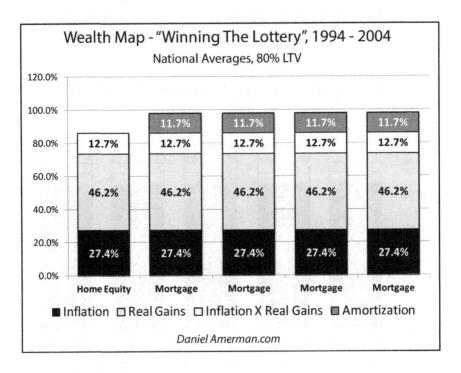

The seventh lottery win switched back to the real market value ticket, and was not quite as large, but when rounded to the nearest whole number, still works to 5X the original 20% home equity. This was for homeowners who bought in 1994, and then experienced a 46.2% real market value gain and a 27.4% inflation gain. When the blocks are strung across the wealth map, then the five primary wealth drivers of the real market gain account for a 231% increase, while the other fourteen sources account for a 247% increase in home equity. This was another very balanced creation of wealth, with the sum of the 14 other sources slightly exceeding the main source of home equity gains.

The total increase in home equity was 478%, which means that home equity increased to about 5.8X its starting amount. Starting equity of $40,000 became $231,200, which is a gain of $191,200. This is now very slightly smaller than the original home price of $200,000 due to the rounding to 5X for the "winning the lottery" definition used herein, but it is likely close enough that most people would take it.

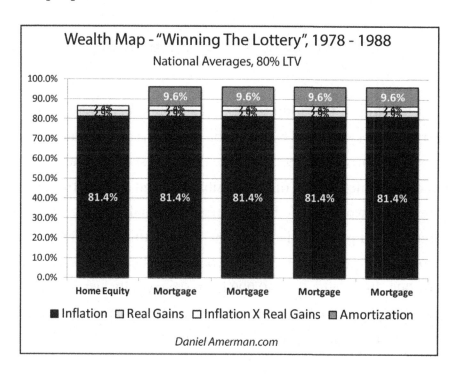

The eighth and final (so far) lottery win flipped back to being based on the inflation ticket, for those who bought homes in 1978. Stringing five 81.4% inflation blocks across the wealth map produced a gain of 407%. Because real price gains were a low 2.9%, this led to a very low secondary wealth creation of just 2.4%, and the total for the other 14 sources of home equity dropped to just 64%.

Nonetheless, the primary wealth driver of inflation was still strong enough that the total increase in home equity was 471%, meaning that the average homeowner would have ended up with 5.7X their original home equity. Starting equity of $40,000 became $228,400 in ten years, which is an $188,400 increase in equity.

A History Of The Extraordinary

Looking at the "lottery wins" as a group, there were 35 ten year periods that ended by 2019, for starting years that ranged from 1975 through 2009. If we take the eight starting years reviewed, which is 23% of the possibilities, and average the gains on equity, it works out to be 5.6 times the initial equity invested. If someone had purchased a $200,000 home with $40,000 in equity, their home equity after ten years would have been an average of $264,000. Removing the $40,000 in starting equity leaves a net gain of $224,000 - which is equal to an average of a little over 110% of the original purchase price of the home.

That does indeed work out to be a 23% chance of experiencing an increase in home equity equal to an average of 110% of the entire purchase price of the home, in the first 10 years.

That is an astonishing upside potential for something that has happened almost a quarter of the time.

It is also just history.

Another way of looking at this is that 24 out of the 35 possible ten year homeownership periods had positive real price gains. This means that all eight levels of the multiplication of wealth were working together 24 times. Out of those 24 times - 8 ten year homeownership periods, or 33% of the total, produced gains on home equity that were about equal to or greater than the entire original purchase price of the home.

That means that so long as real home price gains over ten years were positive at all - history shows the combination of all eight of the levels of the multiplication of wealth working together produces a 1 out of 3 chance of "winning the lottery". There is truly a wealth creation machine at work when all 19 sources of home equity changes are simultaneously positive, that has performed for the homeowners (and real estate investors) of the nation again and again.

Chapter 9

The National Debt & Future Wealth Maps

There is a strong case to be made that if we want to seek the best insights we can find about potential future home prices over the long term - we should then be primarily focusing not on changes in real market value, but changes in inflation. Indeed, history seems quite clear that understanding inflation and what can cause higher rates of inflation has been much more important for the average homeowner experience than just changes in the housing market.

There are reasons to believe that rates of inflation will be changing over the course of the 2020s and 2030s, particularly when compared to the 2000s and 2010s, and that this could become the defining factor for determining the financial advantages of homeownership for the nation as a whole.

The first and most important factor is the relationship between national debts and inflation. The national debt of the United States exploded upwards between 2008 and 2020, and the rate of increase soared to all new levels as the government borrowed the money to try to contain the damage from the shutdowns associated with the attempted containment of the COVID 19 pandemic. Indeed, just in the year 2020, the $4.5 trillion increase in the national debt exceeded the total national debt run up by the United States in its first two centuries of existence, even after adjusting for inflation.

Looking at the government borrowing more in one year than it usually did in two centuries, many people without training in economics may liken the situation to the government being like a person, and having to default at some point. However, governments aren't actually anything like people, given they can create inflation instead of defaulting. And what history shows us is that is exactly what governments do when they get too far into debt (so long as they were able to borrow in their own currency) - they do their best to deliberately create higher rates of inflation.

The government essentially sends a flood of money into the economy over time, greatly decreasing the purchasing power of the dollar. A simplified way of looking at this is to say that the government starts with a $20 trillion national debt, and cuts the value of the dollar in half. That is now relatively speaking a $10 trillion national debt. And if the government halves the value of the dollar again, then what was a $10 trillion national debt effectively becomes a $5 trillion national debt in inflation-adjusted terms.

For savers, and particularly for retirees, this deliberate halving of the purchasing power of savings and then halving again, can be a quite cruel process, slashing standards of living and financial security.

Crucially for homeowners, however, the form that these "halvings" actually take is *a series of doublings.* If in round numbers, a $20 trillion national debt is equal to a $20 trillion dollar economy, then double the number of dollars it takes to buy everything (including homes), and there are now double the tax receipts from a $40 trillion economy to support a $20 trillion debt, making the debt much more affordable for the nation. Then double the number of dollars again - along with the prices of everything (including homes) - and there is now an $80 trillion economy, with the four times increase in taxes from an $80 trillion economy easily paying for a $20 trillion national debt.

That is a vastly oversimplified explanation of a complicated subject - but it is also the essence of how governments deal with large national debts. With national debts jumping upwards around the world, then savers, investors and homeowners really need to be aware of the basics here.

This is where some people jump straight into predicting hyperinflation and the dollar becoming worth a penny in a few years. If hyperinflation were to happen, then the price of a home could quickly rise by ten, fifty or a hundred times, the mortgage would then be insignificant in comparison, and the homeowner would essentially be given the entire value of their home. One aspect of hyperinflation is effectively a massive transfer of wealth from mortgage investors to homeowners who used those mortgages to buy homes, and it is worthwhile to keep this in mind. However, *while it is far better to be the one to whom wealth is transferred than not* - the overall cost of the hyperinflation would be tragic for the nation when it comes to the value of savings, jobs and economic stability.

Hyperinflation can happen, and has happened, but it is fortunately much more the exception rather than the rule. Inflation has frequently slipped out of control in the past, but governments avoided outright hyperinflation the great majority of the time. While the end destination is the same quite thorough destruction of the value of the currency and of savings, the preferred approach for maintaining economic and political stability is to accomplish that destruction over a period of decades rather than in just a few years.

As one example, the United States went heavily into debt to pay for World War II. Over the decades that followed, the long game was that the value of the dollar was halved, and then halved again, and then halved again.

Each time that happened - the long game was that the number of dollars needed to buy most things doubled, and then doubled again, and doubled again, going from $1 to $2 to $4 to $8, in a process that is mathematically identical to compound interest. Those doublings meant that the economy grew much larger - and tax collections grew much larger - relative to the national debt. The flood of new inflated dollars meant that the old dollars of national debt became less important and more affordable.

Each time that happened, all else being equal, the long game of reducing oversized national debts meant that the number of dollars that it took to buy or build homes doubled, and then doubled again, and then doubled again.

As explored in Book 1, the median value of a home in the United States went from $2,900 in 1940, to $11,900 in 1960, to $47,200 in 1980. Meanwhile, the size of the U.S. national debt relative to the economy went from a peak after World War II of 107% in 1947, down to a low of 32% in 1980.

Those numbers are not coincidences and they were the long game of what macroeconomists currently refer to as "financial repression" - the preferred choice of governments trying to control excessively large national debts. This is truly a long game, and may never trigger a daily or annual headline along the way - but it is what happened before, and it could very well be what happens again.

Because of the unequal partnership and the five high stacking - the long game for controlling large national debts was extraordinarily profitable for the average homeowner in the past.

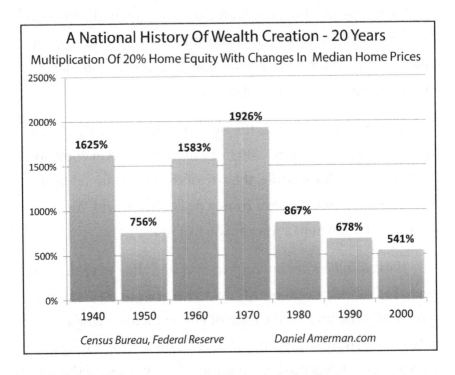

As explored in Book 1, a 20% starting home equity in 1940 on a $2,900 median value home would have increased by 16X as homes rose to a median value of $11,900 by 1960, even without including mortgage amortization. A starting 20% home equity in 1960 on an $11,900 home would have also increased by about 16X by 1980 as homes rose to a median value of $47,200.

What is most important to keep in mind about those successive 16X gains over the long term – is that they weren't about timing the market, or making brilliant investment decisions, or gambling or speculation. They were about alignment with government policies and the financial interests of a government that was heavily in debt. This fundamental alignment was the natural byproduct of buying a home with a mortgage, and it existed whether or not the homeowner had any idea of what they were doing when they bought that four bedroom house in a good neighborhood with the particularly nice kitchen.

No one can know the particulars of the years ahead, or what market or political changes may be coming, let alone the impact of any future wars, pandemics or technological revolutions that may be on the way. The future always seems to end up being a surprise, after all. Yet, that said, we have been through numerous wars, radical political and geopolitical changes, market crashes, and technological revolutions since 1940, and the long game beneath it all - was the successive doubling of the dollars needed to buy most things, and the doubling again, and the doubling again.

As of the beginning of the 2020s, the U.S. government was heavily, heavily indebted and the situation was rapidly getting worse. There is therefore every reason to anticipate that over the years and decades ahead, the government will deliberately create higher rates of inflation, as they have in the past, for the self-serving reason that higher rates of inflation are much less politically costly than the alternatives for dealing with huge debts, such as sky high tax rates lasting for decades, or outright default.

The particulars can never be precisely known in advance in terms of the years, or the annual inflation rates, or the actual length of time for the number of dollars to double. But even if we don't know the exact particulars for any year or five year span - governments using higher rates of inflation to manage large national debts is in no way a random or market process. The long game over the decades for heavily indebted nations is the doubling of the number of dollars to buy everything, and then the doubling again, in a relentless, cumulative, one way and highly reliable process.

This cruel process for savers does create a long, slow and quite reliable long game for average homeowners as well, where the values of homes double and then double again - *just as we have seen in the past* - with a multiplication and stacking of those inflation doublings occurring for homeowners with mortgages over the years as well, as the natural result of being in that position in such an environment.

Future 1: Three Percent Inflation

The potential implications for homeowners of a very large national debt can be explored by using round number illustrations and wealth maps. These are not predictions, but we can use what we have learned about the past in the previous seventeen chapters of Books 1 & 2, in order to explore how some of these factors could combine to potentially impact the Homeowner Wealth Formula in the future. For a starting base case, we will look at what happens if the U.S. national debt does not lead to higher rates of inflation.

1. Compounded Inflation. Looking at 44 years of historical data, a 3.6% annual rate of inflation when fed into the compound interest formula produced the historical increase in price levels between 1975 and 2019. This was not uniform in practice but rather the annual rates of inflation varied quite a bit in the past, as may very well be true in the future.

A round number and somewhat lower rate of inflation for the future - assuming no issues or influence from the national debt - would be a 3% annual average rate of inflation. Using the compound interest formula, multiplying 103% times itself 30 times in a row leads to price levels of 243% in 30 years, which is a 143% increase in price relative to today.

2. National Debt. A very simple way of looking at a complex problem is that if price levels rise to 243% of where they are today just from inflation, then the economy grows to 243% of its current size over 30 years (even without including economic growth), and taxes also rise to 243% of the tax collections today, all else being equal. Because there are 243% of the tax dollars, the cost of paying for the old national debt is only about 41% of what it used to be (100% / 243% = 41%). This is not huge for 30 years, but this 59% reduction in the starting real national debt over time is a key part of the reason why governments with large national debts have policies of creating steady annual rates of inflation.

3. Savers. For a saver to maintain purchasing power, they will need to have 143% more dollars in 30 years than they have now. If they have anything less, then they are losing part of the purchasing power of their savings, and becoming poorer in real terms. If the saver does not have any protection against inflation, then the same increase in price levels that drops the real cost of the national debt down to 41% over 30 years, also drops the real value of their savings down to 41% of the value today.

4. Home Prices (First & Second Levels). Historically, there has been a close relationship between home prices and inflation, with inflation being by far the dominant influence on home prices over the long term. If we start with a $225,000 home, there is one year of 3% inflation, and the house keeps up with inflation - the home price will rise to $231,750. This is the first level of the multiplication of wealth.

When this happens for 30 years in a row, then we multiply 103% times itself 30 times, which equals 243%, and the value of the home in 30 years now equals about $547,000. This is the second level of the multiplication of wealth, and history shows that this has been historically reliable in solving the saver's dilemma. The saver faces the dilemma of how to have 243% of their starting dollars, and homeownership has historically delivered the needed new dollars, protecting against inflation.

5. Home Equity With Mortgage. (Third Level).

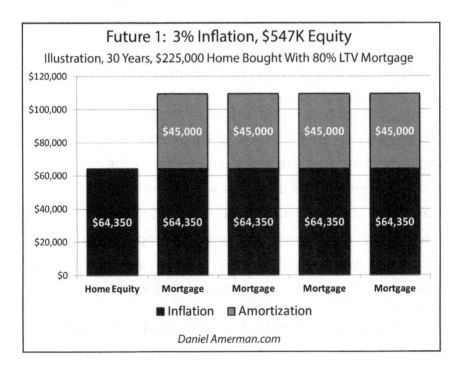

When the $225,000 home is bought with an 80% LTV mortgage, then the starting home equity is $45,000. Keeping up with inflation would require a 143% inflation gain on that home equity, which would be equal to $64,350. Because of the unequal partnership, the homeowner would also own the four $64,350 inflation gains associated with the mortgage lender's four $45,000 funding buckets.

The homeowner of the future would turn inflation into wealth, as have generations of homeowners in the past. In this case, $45,000 in starting equity would have all the rights to $321,750 in inflation gains on the home, far exceeding the destruction of the value of the dollar.

The natural flow of wealth from this third level of the multiplication of wealth, is to take the 59% reduction in the real value of the old national debt, and the 59% reduction in the real value of savings, and flip them into a 715% home equity gain. This is with just moderate inflation, and no real price gains.

6. Paying Off Mortgage (Fourth Level). As the result of making 30 years of mortgage payments instead of rental payments, the homeowner would entirely pay off the mortgage. (There is also the huge benefit of avoiding a 143% increase in rents over the years, as covered in Book 3 of this series.)

The four funding buckets of $45,000 each would have been entirely repaid. The homeowner would now never need to make another mortgage payment, but would own their now $547,000 home free and clear. A starting equity of $45,000 would have become $547,000, or 12.2X the starting equity as the natural result of buying a home with a mortgage.

Once the mortgage is gone, we can also do a bit of a simplification. We have the home equity we started with, multiplied times five because we own 100% of a home instead of 20%, and that is then multiplied by compounded inflation.

We start with $45,000 in equity and 20% of the home, we multiply times five to get $225,000 because we now own 100% of the home outright, and we then multiply times 243% because of compounded inflation, to get a home value of about $547,000.

This is not how the numbers work before the mortgage is paid off. As explored in Chapters 4 through 7 of Book 1 in particular, amortization and paying down the mortgage aren't necessarily particularly important when it comes to turning inflation into wealth with a home and a mortgage in the early years of ownership. However, while the simplification does not explain how wealth was created while the mortgage was outstanding, it is a useful shortcut once the mortgage is gone.

Future 2: Six Percent Inflation

For the next round number illustration, we will assume that a U.S. government struggling to control the financial effects of very large national debt does use substantially higher rates of inflation. While the rates are likely to vary widely over the years, we will assume that it works out to a six percent annual average rate of inflation.

1. Compounded Inflation. Using the compound interest formula, multiplying 106% times itself 30 times in a row leads to price levels of 574% in 30 years, which is a 474% increase in price relative to today.

2. National Debt. A very simple way of looking at a complex problem is that if price levels rise to 574% of where they are today just from inflation, then the economy grows to 574% of its current size over 30 years (even without including economic growth), and taxes also rise to 574% of the tax collections today, all else being equal. Because there are 574% of the tax dollars, the cost of paying for the old national debt is only about 17% of what it used to be (100% / 574% = 17%).

Bringing in 574% of the taxes and thereby achieving an 83% reduction in the starting real national debt is indicative of a far more serious effort to pay for and contain the debt, and is consistent with the much larger national debt in the early 2020s than what was seen when inflation was averaging about 3.6% per year.

3. Savers. For a saver to maintain purchasing power, they will need to have 474% more dollars in 30 years than they have now. If they have anything less, then they are losing part of the purchasing power of their savings, and becoming poorer in real terms. The particulars of just what the personal strategies are that the saver uses to create the new dollars to keep up with inflation are now becoming very important. If the saver does not have any strategies or any protection against inflation, then the same increase in price levels that drops the real cost of the national debt down to 17% over 30 years, also drops the real value of their savings down to 17% of the value today.

4. Home Prices (First & Second Levels). If we start with a $225,000 home, there is one year of 6% inflation, and the house keeps up with inflation - the home price rises to $238,500, in the first level of the multiplication of wealth.

When this happens for 30 years in a row, then we multiply 106% times itself 30 times, which equals 574%, and the value of the home in 30 years now equals about $1,291,500, which is almost $1.3 million.

When we look at the difference in the home prices between 3% and 6% inflation rates, then we see a possible future version of the historical power of the compound interest formula over home prices. A 3% rate of inflation produced only a $349,000 home price increase over 30 years. A six percent annual rate of inflation is only twice that of a three percent rate of inflation - but yet when it is compounded inside the compound interest formula for 30 years, it produces a $1,066,500 increase in home prices, which is 3.3 times as great as the increase with 3% inflation.

5. Home Equity With Mortgage. (Third Level).

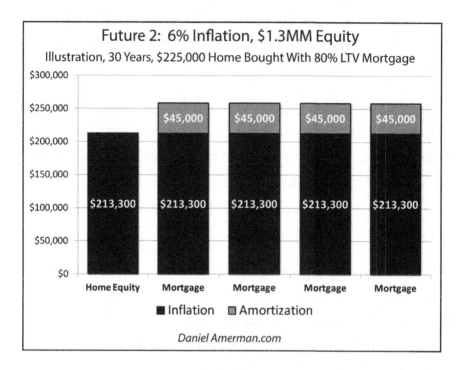

With a 6% annually compounded rate of inflation, the 474% inflation gain on the $45,000 in starting home equity would equal $213,300. Because the home was bought with a mortgage, we would then run a string of five $213,300 blocks across the wealth map, totaling $1,066,500.

The homeowner of the future would turn inflation into wealth, with $45,000 in starting equity having the rights to all $1,066,500 in future inflation gains.

The natural flow of wealth from this third level of the multiplication of wealth, is to take the 83% reduction in the real value of the national debt, and the 83% reduction in the real value of savings, and flip them into a 2770% home equity gain. When we materially increase the power of the compound interest formula, and then multiply that exponential increase in power because of the mortgage, we can start to get to some spectacular numbers in terms of the increase in home equity.

6. Paying Off Mortgage (Fourth Level). The four funding buckets of $45,000 each would have been entirely repaid, and the 474% increase in rent payments over the years would have been dodged. *A starting equity of $45,000 would have become about $1.3 million, or 28.7 times the starting equity as the natural result of buying a home with a mortgage.*

When the mortgage has paid off, because the real market value of the home hasn't changed but the homeowner now owns all five funding buckets, we multiply times five, and there is a 5X increase in real home equity, explaining 17% of the 28.7X increase in home equity. The other 83% of the home equity increase is the result of successfully keeping up with inflation and owning the results for all five of the funding buckets.

If the long term rate of inflation does rise to something like 6% because of a huge and growing national debt, then we could also see an increasing divergence between theory and real world financial security for the average person. A little over $1 million of the $1.3 million price in 30 years for what is a $225,000 home today would be just the result of inflation. An economic theoretician might wave their hand in annoyance and make the $1 million disappear, because it is "just" inflation, and it disappears when we run the mathematical formula for calculating inflation-adjusted dollars.

On the other hand, for someone in the real world who bought that home - they would have the additional $1 million as the natural flow of wealth from buying a nice place to live their life in, and of having paid for most of the original purchase price with a mortgage. Looking at the price of their home at that time, the more than $1 million would indeed be 83% of the net worth they have in home equity.

If they hadn't bought the house and then had the $1 million arrive over the long term as the natural byproduct of owning a home with a mortgage in a time of higher inflation - as a matter of real people, real knowledge, and real human behavior, how much of that $1 million (or $1.3 million) would that person be likely to have?

As explored in Chapter 1 of Book1, when we look at the national medians, then most people don't do as well in practice as they are supposed to, if they were following the most common advice. They often don't set up any intentional long term savings or wealth strategy at all, if they do they don't fund it as much as they are "supposed" to, and they may not make the theoretically best decisions for how to grow that money.

So, in practice, a renter might not have any of that extra $1 million (or $1.3 million) in extra net worth in 30 years, or they might have only a small fraction of it. For the typical person in practice - they are unlikely to set up, fund, and consistently execute over 30 years a sophisticated financial plan for keeping up with potentially higher rates of inflation.

This means that for many people in the actual world that we live in - the additional $1 million would be there if they bought the home, and it wouldn't be if they didn't. That makes the $1 million entirely real for those people. Now, it wouldn't have the purchasing power that $1 million does today - but it would likely still be the largest component of their net worth at that time.

The issue is that there is more than one perspective on "reality". With 30 years of compounded 6% inflation the future dollars are worth much less than current dollars, so it wouldn't be fair to say they are all true gains. The economic theoretician is absolutely correct in that regard.

On the other hand, there is a split that occurs in the real world, between those who lead lives where they have a large amount of net worth that is naturally growing with the power of inflation inside of the compound interest formula, with no further effort on their part - and those who don't. For many people, the vast majority of the money they might have in 30 years could be the result of this participation - and that has the natural result of creating a truly life changing amount of net worth and financial security over the decades, an additional $1 million with this round number illustration. That $1 million likely wouldn't exist at all or would be a much smaller amount for the typical person who was not a homeowner.

This same relationship is plainly visible when we look at the present and past. About 35% of homeowners own their home free and clear, and it is likely fair to say that they are mostly older. Inflation over 30 years accounted for about $115,000 out of the $225,000 median value for a home in 2019, even with the lower inflation rates of the 2000s and 2010s. For the typical older homeowner, it is likely fair to say that is $115,000 they have in net worth because they were homeowners, and $115,000 they were unlikely to have if they were not homeowners

Future 3: Nine Percent Inflation

As of 2020, the United States government is arguably in the worst shape that it has ever been when it comes to the national debt. It isn't just the record setting numbers in terms of dollars or relative to the economy. A potentially even worse problem is the indefinite projected growth in future budget deficits. When the national debt previously soared, it was from paying for the costs of World War II, and when the war stopped so did the record deficits. The government was then able to use inflation to gradually bring the debt back under control in a disciplined process, over a period of decades.

Starting from a record level of debt - and then projecting record deficits into the future with the no cure or plan in sight, means that the debt becomes unsolvable. There is no fiscal discipline, just unending growth in the debt. Unless... the traditional cure of inflation is used. The problem is that the greater the national debt problem, the higher the rate of inflation that may eventually be needed to cure it. For this third round number illustration, we will use a 9% annual rate of inflation.

1. Compounded Inflation. Using the compound interest formula, multiplying 109% times itself 30 times in a row leads to price levels of 1327% in 30 years, which is a 1227% increase in price relative to today. Because it is based on an exponential function, the compound interest formula grows vastly more powerful with higher rates of inflation.

2. National Debt. Returning to a very simple way of looking at a complex problem, if price levels rise to 1327% of where they are today just from inflation, then the economy grows to 1327% of its current size over 30 years (even without including economic growth), and taxes also rise to 1327% of the tax collections today, all else being equal. Because there are 1327% of the tax dollars, the cost of paying for the old national debt is only about 7.5% of what it used to be (100% / 1327% = 7.5%).

Bringing in 1327% of the taxes and thereby achieving a 92.5% reduction in the starting real national debt is a powerhouse move that is indeed indicative of a true national debt emergency - and in combination with other measures may be capable of dealing with such an emergency.

3. Savers. It is the savers who pay the greatest price for a national debt crisis when extraordinary measures are used. For a saver to maintain purchasing power, they will need to have 1227% more dollars in 30 years than they have now. If they have anything less, then they are losing part of the purchasing power of their savings, and becoming poorer in real terms.

How will they do that? For methods other than homeownership, the particulars of just what the personal strategies are that the saver uses to create the new dollars to keep up with inflation are now extremely important. If the saver does not have any strategies or any protection against inflation, then the same increase in price levels that drops the real cost of the national debt down to 7.5% over 30 years, also drops the real value of their savings down to 7.5% of the value today.

4. Home Prices (First & Second Levels). If we start with a $225,000 home, there is one year of 9% inflation, and the house keeps up with inflation - then the home price rises to $245,250, in the first level of the multiplication of wealth.

When this happens for 30 years in a row, then we multiply 109% times itself 30 times, which equals 1327%, and the value of the home in 30 years now equals $2,986,000, which is about $3 million.

When we look at the difference in the home prices between 3% and 9% inflation rates, then we see a possible future version of how the compound interest formula can come to completely dominate home prices. In any given year, 9% inflation will only produce 3X the home price increase that a 3% rate of inflation would. However, when we have the successive multiplications of 109% times itself inside the compound interest formula, then we get a $2.8 million home price increase, instead of a $349,000 home price increase. Over 30 years, a 9% annual rate of inflation will lead to a home price increase that is about 8X greater than the increase from a 3% rate of inflation.

5. Home Equity With Mortgage. (Third Level).

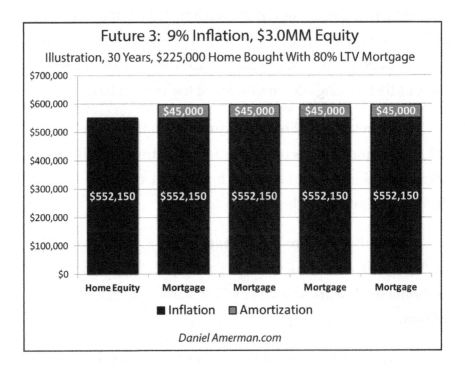

With a 9% annually compounded rate of inflation, the 1227% inflation gain on the $45,000 in starting home equity would equal $552,150. Because the home was bought with a mortgage, we would then run a string of five $552,150 blocks across the wealth map, totaling $2,761,000, or about $2.8 million.

The homeowner of the future would turn inflation into wealth, with $45,000 in starting equity having the rights to all $2.8 million in future inflation gains.

The natural flow of wealth from this third level of the multiplication of wealth is to take the 92.5% reduction in the real value of the national debt, and the 92.5% reduction in the real value of savings, and flip them into a 6535% gain on homeowner equity. When we vastly increase the power of the compound interest formula, and then multiply that exponential increase in power because of the mortgage, we can get an absolutely amazing result.

6. Paying Off Mortgage (Fourth Level). The four funding buckets of $45,000 each would have been entirely repaid, and the 1227% increase in rent payments over the years would have been dodged. A starting equity of $45,000 would have become about $3 million, or 66.3X the starting equity as the natural result of buying a home with a mortgage.

When the mortgage has paid off, because the real market value of the home hasn't changed but the homeowner now owns all five funding buckets, we multiply times five, and there is a 5X increase in real home equity, then paying off the mortgage explains only 7.5% of the 66.3X increase in home equity. The other 92.5% of the home equity increase is the result of successfully keeping up with inflation and owning the results for all five of the funding buckets.

With a 9% annual rate of inflation compounded for 30 years, then about $2.8 million out of the $3 million future price of what would be a $225,000 home today would be solely the result of inflation. An economic theoretician might get downright upset at the idea of anyone considering any of that $2.8 million to be real, because it is "just" inflation, and it disappears when we run the mathematical formula for calculating inflation-adjusted dollars. After all, the home costs $3 million because a hamburger and fries now costs over $100.

But yet, in the real world, some people will have that $2.8 million - and others will not.

The higher the national debt is relative to the economy and taxes, then the higher the future rates of inflation that are likely to be needed to bring it back under control (all else being equal). The higher the future rates of inflation, then the more important that the compound interest formula becomes when determining the future prices of everything - including homes. The math rules, as it has in the past, and this is true whether the general public realizes this is the case, or not.

Taking it to the next level, the higher the national debt, the bigger the likely future split in financial security between those who are benefiting from the power of the compound interest formula, and those who are being savaged by the power of the compound interest formula. A homeowner would be multiplying their dollars, year after year, becoming a millionaire and then a multimillionaire.

True - being a millionaire won't mean what it means today, let alone what it meant 30 or 50 years ago. But in a world where the cost of a burger and fries is up over $100, it is much better to be a multimillionaire than to not be one.

As the saying goes: "history doesn't repeat itself, but it does rhyme". We've seen something like this happen before, it isn't just theory and speculation, and the results were life changing for a nation. For a different set of reasons, the United States did go through a period of much higher inflation rates in the 1970s and early 1980s.

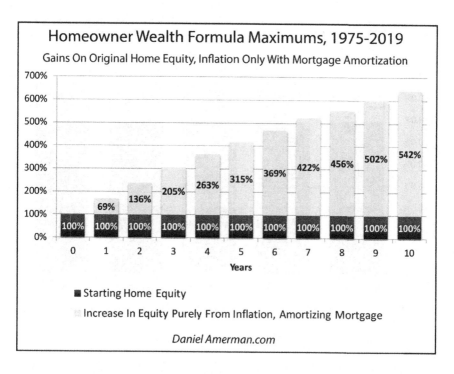

Looking just at the historical inflation peaks from the 1970s and early 1980s, as well as mortgage amortizations, the natural average result for homeowners was to see their home equity triple in just three years, quadruple in five years, quintuple in seven years, and increase by 6X in nine years. Keep in mind as well that those are just short term numbers, and that the compound interest formula does become exponentially more powerful with more time to work with, such as 20 years, 30 years, or more.

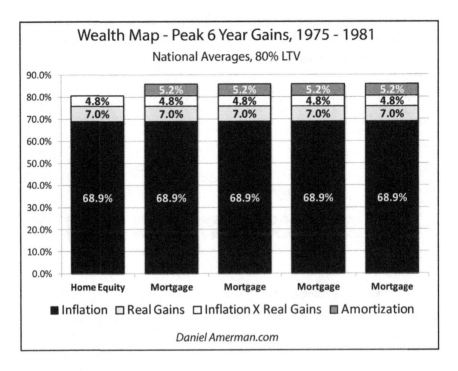

As explored in Chapter 8, four of the eight examples of "winning the lottery" were the results of higher rates of inflation producing national average results where home equity increased by an amount about equal to the entire original home purchase price in just ten years.

If a record high and still surging national debt does eventually lead to materially higher rates of inflation over the coming decades than what we have seen in recent decades, then the underlying math of the Homeowner Wealth Formula shows us that there is likely to be an amplification of the creation of wealth to higher levels than what we have historically experienced to date.

What is also likely to be amplified is the difference in life outcomes when it comes to standard of living and financial security, between those who are homeowners and those who are not. We can look at this on three different levels.

The first level is real or inflation-adjusted dollars. What starts as $45,000 in purchasing power becomes $225,000 in purchasing power. That is technically correct, it is very difficult to do, and it would be an amazing accomplishment over decades of higher inflation rates, when most people are unable to keep up with inflation at all when it comes to savings.

The second level reflects financial reality, life choices, and just how difficult it is to make a financial plan, actually fund it and do it, and then keep it going successfully for three decades. Most people will not do that in practice - but for the homeowner, it is the natural byproduct of owning a home with a mortgage. The real world difference for a homeowner in three decades with 9% compounded inflation is owning a $3 million home free and clear in a world where a burger and fries goes for over $100, whereas the renter probably won't have the $3 million but will still be living in a world where a burger and fries costs over $100.

The third level is more the subject of the next book, but some key aspects are valid - and potentially life changing for this round number illustration. If rent rises with a 9% rate of inflation, then rent is 50% higher after five years, 100% higher after eight years, 200% higher after 13 years, 300% higher after 16 years, 400% higher after 19 years, 500% higher after 21 years, and so forth, as the rent accelerates upwards with the exponential power of the compound interest formula. If the renter wants to keep a roof over their head, they had better hope that their income is also accelerating upwards with the power of the compound interest formula.

Meanwhile, for the homeowner, the principal and interest component of their mortgage payment is not rising at all (the escrows for insurance and taxes are a different matter). If their income is rising with inflation - then each year, their mortgage payment uses up less and less of their monthly income. The longer the compound interest formula has time to run, then the smaller the amount of their income that is needed to pay the mortgage, and the greater the percentage of their income that is freed up for increased standard of living and building financial security.

The homeowner has a $3 million home in 30 years, and the mortgage payment stops altogether, after having become increasingly insignificant with each passing year. The renter may have nothing after 30 years, and would have just spent the previous 30 years scrambling to find ways to pay their fast rising rent payments, perhaps depleting what savings they had in the process. So in 30 years and 1 month, the renter would have to come up with a rent payment that is 1327% of their initial rent payment (about $16,000 per month for what would be a $1,200 rent today), as they would have to do in each future month as rents continued to rise, while the homeowner - would not.

While not the subject of this particular book, it is worth noting that the implications are stunning for real estate investors, as covered in my video course and workshops. The combination of soaring investment equity, fixed mortgage payments and soaring rental payments can create not just a refuge from inflation, but an ability to financially prosper from high rates of inflation that is very difficult to find anywhere else.

If the soaring and out of control national debt does lead to materially higher inflation rates over the coming years and decades, then there is a very strong case to be made that the single most important financial decision that will be made by a individual or a family is whether to do what it takes to become homeowners - or not.

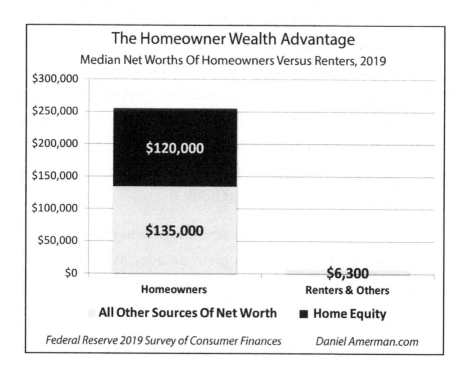

When we look at the forty to one median net worth advantage of homeowners over renters in 2019, we can see the impact of all these elements for the household in the middle, the median households where half of all households have more net worth and half have less. The household in the middle won't be a new homeowner but they generally won't be one of the older households either. This means that they are likely mostly middle aged homeowners and would have had a number of years to benefit, but they won't have yet reached the maximum benefits stage.

The direct combination of turning inflation into wealth, and having a large asset that is keeping up step by step with the inflationary compounding of dollars, is enough to produce home equity that is almost half of net worth. If the years of mortgage payments that didn't rise as rents did are taken into account, and the savings and asset purchases that occurred with the money that was freed up are also taken into account, then homeownership likely accounts for well over half of household net worth for many of those households in the middle. (Refinancings that have taken advantage of falling interest rates to actually reduce mortgage payments have been a further source of advantage and net worth, but again, that is more for the next book.)

The extraordinary financial advantages to homeowners already exist and have existed for many decades, as has the life changing importance of the homeownership decision for the typical person or family.

If we do see higher rates of inflation, whether from the soaring national debt or other sources altogether, then we will see not a new source of wealth, but a potentially powerful amplification of an existing and proven source of wealth. However, because home prices would be rising with the power of the compound interest formula, and the results of that exponential equation would then be multiplied again when the home is purchased with a mortgage - the new degree to which wealth would multiply is not intuitive for most people, and could be called astonishing.

A 92.5% destruction of the purchasing power of the dollar over 30 years translates to a 6535% gain on home equity, as $45,000 becomes $3 million, because... that's just the math of the Homeowner Wealth Formula.

Chapter 10

Population Growth & Future Wealth Maps

There has been another long term process of multiplication underway, and that is the multiplication of population. The population of the United States was about 132 million as of the 1940 census, and was estimated to be about 331 million as of late 2020. Even as median home values rose from $2,900 to $225,000, an increase of over $220,000, the U.S. population increased by almost 200 million people.

As developed in Chapter 2 of Book 1, there are self-correcting economic forces that generally keep home prices rising at a rate that is not that far from the rate of inflation. If home prices go up more than the rate of inflation, then homes can be built for less than what they can be sold for, and home builders will build until supply meets demand. If home prices increase less than the rate of inflation, then homes can't be sold for what it costs to build them, and builders stop building until supply meets demand.

However, that only holds true so long as: A) undeveloped land is available within a reasonable commuting distance of where the work is; and B) regulatory burdens are not excessive.

The United States is a vast country, but where people live has been shifting. An ever greater percentage of a much larger population has been concentrating in selected urban areas, near the coasts, and in the southern half of the nation. Particularly in places like California, the supply of undeveloped land in commuting range of major cities is almost out, and regulatory costs have been rising fast. These are the type of pressures that lead to increases in real market values, where home prices rise faster than the rate of inflation.

These are long term market and demographic forces, with many complexities. However, all else being equal and over the long term, so long as trends continue of increasing population and an increasing concentration of that population in selected areas, then that should produce an upwards pressure on real market values for homes.

We have two primary wealth drivers for the homeowner wealth maps, inflation and real market value changes. A fast climbing and huge national debt is likely to require higher rates of inflation at some point, increasing one wealth driver. A growing and possibly still concentrating population may increase the other main wealth driver.

Both primary wealth drivers are multiplicative when a home is bought with a mortgage. Crucially, each are multiplied by the other - and the resulting increase in wealth is then multiplied again, if the home was bought with a mortgage.

Future 4: 3% Inflation, 50% Real Market Value Increase

Each of the factors of a growing population, increasing concentration of population, increasing regulatory burdens and increasing affordability due to very low interest rates could also be called long term multipliers of a sort, although not as quantifiable or as reliable as inflation or amortization.

If the future does turn out to hold still more population increases, with a disproportionate amount of that growth in a few regions, even while the supply and costs of new homes are impacted by increasing regulations - there is a very good chance that those factors in combination could be fundamental sources of long term increases in real home prices.

To better understand what this could mean for home prices and homeowner wealth in the future, we need to better understand the past, and we do have a guide in the form of the long term wealth map to show us the implications.

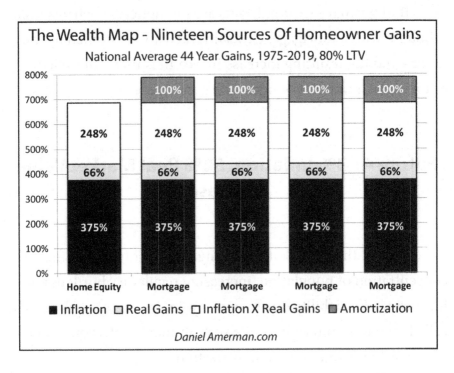

The Wealth Map - Nineteen Sources Of Homeowner Gains
National Average 44 Year Gains, 1975-2019, 80% LTV

As explored in Chapter 5, the 66% increase in real home market values by itself accounted for only 1.7% of the total almost 40 to 1 increase in home equity between 1975 and 2019. Yet, a full 41% of the surface area of the long term wealth map, 41% of the total wealth creation, was dependent on that little "seed" and the 24 to 1 multiplication of that seed through the combination of the sixth, seventh and eighth levels of the multiplication of wealth.

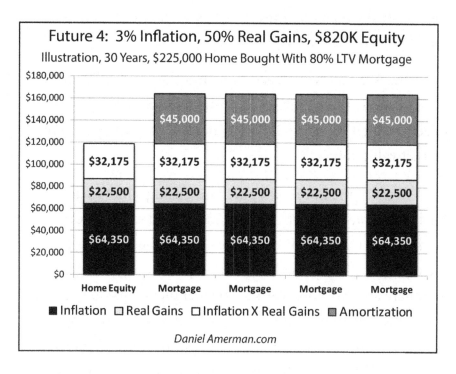

Future 4: 3% Inflation, 50% Real Gains, $820K Equity
Illustration, 30 Years, $225,000 Home Bought With 80% LTV Mortgage

■ Inflation ☐ Real Gains ☐ Inflation X Real Gains ■ Amortization

Daniel Amerman.com

To return to our round number illustrations (not predictions), if a soaring national debt does not turn out to materially increase inflation, and we have a compounded 3% rate of inflation over 30 years, then it takes 143% more dollars to buy everything, and that produces a home price increase of 143%. Now, let's say that over those same 30 years, the combination of population growth and other factors leads to a national average round number 50% increase in real, inflation-adjusted home values.

In dollar terms, a 50% increase in home values would lead to a 50% increase in the starting home equity of $45,000 for a $225,000 median value home purchased with an 80% LTV mortgage. This is the fifth level of the multiplication of wealth, it equals $22,500, and can be seen in the leftmost column which represents the portion of the home purchase price that was funded by homeowner equity.

The $22,500 is the "seed", which is then multiplied by the sixth, seventh and eighth levels of the multiplication of wealth to get the total home equity price increases resulting from real market value gains.

Because the home was purchased using a mortgage, the homeowner also gets the real market value gains from the four mortgage funding buckets. This is the sixth level of the multiplication of wealth, the multiplication of real gains, and there are therefore five $22,500 real market gains strung across the wealth map, for a total of $112,500. In inflation-adjusted terms, the total impact of the fifth and sixth levels of multiplication is to see home equity increase by 250%, or 2.5 times.

However, it takes 143% more dollars to buy everything in 30 years. So to get the eventual price impact for the portion of the home purchased with equity, we need to multiply the $22,500 real gain by 143%. This is an additional $32,175 in dollars that will be there in 30 years, and it is the seventh level of the multiplication of wealth.

Now, those 32,175 dollars do "disappear" if we divide back by inflation to get to current dollars, but in 30 years they would be as real as any other dollars, and someone who had those dollars because of their homeownership decision would indeed have a major financial advantage over someone who didn't have those dollars, because they made a different decision.

This is particularly true when the home was purchased with a mortgage, and the homeowner gets the inflation gains associated with all five of the real market gains, as the eighth level of the multiplication of wealth. Multiplying times five turns a $32,175 gain into about a total $161,875 inflation gain for the homeowner.

When we assemble on the wealth map all of the boxes associated with real market value gains, there are two rows of five each, as developed in Chapter 5 and our study of the past. Those same relationships would produce ten boxes in the future so long as we have both inflation gains and real price gains. The total dollars for the ten boxes would be $273,375, which is 12.1X as great as the $22,500 "seed" of real market value gains on starting home equity.

This is a critical relationship. If we look at the population growth factors in isolation - that is a .5 or 50% increase, $22,500 on $45,000 in equity. If that increase occurs during a time of 3% inflation and the home was bought with a mortgage, then that real gain is multiplied times 12.1 for a total of $273,000. The starting real gain is only 8.2% of the total increase in home price.

When the $273,000 that is dependent on real market value gains is added to the $547,000 in home equity for 3% inflation and mortgage amortization that was developed in the previous chapter, then the total home value - and home equity once the mortgage is gone - is now $820,000. *This represents a 1723% gain on the original equity of $45,000.*

On a fundamental basis, population growth and other factors can multiply home prices, those gains are multiplied again when there is compounded inflation, and the resulting gains are multiplied again when the home was bought with a mortgage.

With our round number illustrations of a 3% inflation rate and a 50% long term increase in real home values, then about 33% of the wealth map, and about 33% of the $820,000 home price would be based on the increase in real home values. This can also be seen when we look at the simplification that can be done once the mortgage is gone.

In inflation-adjusted dollars, once the mortgage is gone, then the homeowner started out putting up the cash for 20% of the home and they end up with 100% of a home, in a 5X increase - that has a far higher price because of successfully keeping up with inflation. When the home goes up to 150% of its original value, then the 5X increase becomes a 7.5X increase in inflation-adjusted dollars - that leads to an even higher home price with the additional levels of multiplication.

To keep up with inflation, even at moderate levels, is a highly attractive result. To not just fully keep up with inflation, but to exceed that standard by 7.5X over is an outstanding result. We can look at this as a 1723% gain on the starting home equity investment, or a 7.5X increase in inflation-adjusted equity, and both are accurate. The 1723% gain looks great and is by far the most common perspective. For the smaller number of people used to working with inflation-adjusted dollars, the 7.5X increase is actually even more impressive. Either way, the results of future real market value increases can bring a multiplication of wealth for homeowners.

Future 5: 6% Inflation, 50% Real Market Value Increase

When we look at the enormous and growing size of the U.S. national debt, and consider the possibility of a 6% rate of inflation over the coming years - then our fifth and sixth levels of the multiplication of wealth do not change.

If we assume that population growth and other factors increase real home values by 50% over the next 30 years, then we still have a $22,500 gain on the original home equity, and because the home was bought with a mortgage, five of those gains are strung across the wealth map for a total gain of $112,500.

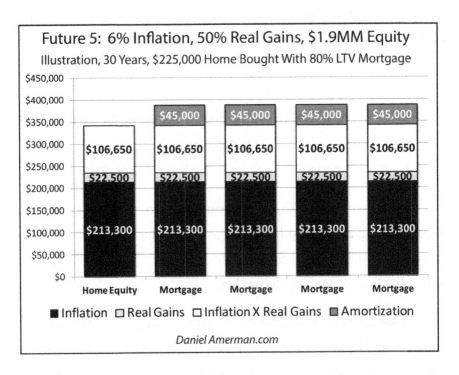

Future 5: 6% Inflation, 50% Real Gains, $1.9MM Equity
Illustration, 30 Years, $225,000 Home Bought With 80% LTV Mortgage

Because it now takes 474% more dollars to buy everything in 30 years, that means we need to multiply our real gains of $22,500 on starting home equity by 474%. That adds another $106,650 block in our starting home equity column, in the seventh level of the multiplication of wealth. Because the home was bought with a mortgage, there are a string of five such blocks, for a total of $533,250, in the eighth level of the multiplication of wealth.

The additional half million in price and home equity gains on $45,000 in starting equity has a fairly fascinating source. This isn't the exact equation of course, but the essence of it is that we are multiplying the impact of the growth in the national debt by the impact of the growth in the population, and "KABOOM!", the price of an average home just went up by an additional half million dollars.

The growth in the national debt creates the need for higher rates of inflation, if the debt is to be kept from spiraling out of control and effectively financially consuming the nation. When the higher rates of inflation are fed into the compound interest formula, a veritable flood of new dollars is created, for both tax revenues - and home prices.

At the same time, a complex of factors may be coming together to increase home prices over the coming decades. Increasing population concentrates in areas with very limited land, boosting prices, even while what new building is done to fulfill the housing needs of a growing population faces increasing regulatory burdens, also boosting prices. Another part of the national debt may wrap around here as well, as large national debts require low interest rates, which increases affordability, and allows home prices to climb still further.

The surge in real prices from population growth is then multiplied by the flood of new dollars from the growth in the national debt - and an additional half million dollar increase in home equity is the result, with our round number illustration of a starting $225,000 home, a 6% rate of inflation, and a 50% increase in real home values over 30 years.

When we add up all ten blocks associated with the fifth through eighth layers of the multiplication of wealth, they now total $645,750 in additional gains. This is now 28.7 times greater than the $22,500 "seed" of the real gains on the starting home equity, thanks to the greater power of the compound interest formula.

The higher rate of inflation radically changes the multiplication of real gains. If we look at the population growth factors in isolation - that is a .5 or 50% increase, $22,500 on $45,000 in equity. If that increase occurs during a time of 6% inflation and the home was bought with a mortgage, then whatever the real gain was is multiplied times 28.7 and the starting real gain is down to only 3.5% of the total increase in home price.

When we add those $645,750 in gains to the $1,291,500 base home price for 6% inflation and amortization developed in the previous chapter, we get a new total home price of $1,937,250, which is not all that far away from a $2 million home. *Including all eight levels of the multiplication of wealth gets us up to a 4205% gain in home equity, going from $45,000 in starting equity, say at age 30, up to a little less than a $2 million home owned outright by age 60.* (This can also be looked at as a $2 million rental property owned outright by age 80, if purchased with $45,000 down at age 50.)

Future 6: 9% Inflation, 50% Real Market Value Increase

As of the writing of this book, there was no solution or end in sight for what the government itself was projecting to be staggering annual budget deficits running through the 2020s,

2030s and beyond, with each year adding another $1+ trillion to the national debt. The national debt may still just be getting going compared to where it could be in ten or fifteen years.

This situation hasn't been seen before in the U.S., and keeping it at least somewhat under control could require sustained rates of inflation that are materially higher than the long term norms - such as a 9% rate of inflation.

With a round number 9% illustration, population growth and related issues would still produce the same fifth and sixth levels of the multiplication of wealth, with a $22,500 real market value gain on original equity, being strung across the wealth map because of the mortgage, with total real gains of $112,5000, that are equal to 250% of starting equity.

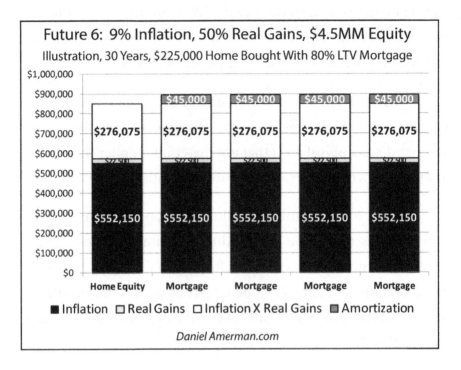

The flood of new dollars that result from 9% annual inflation that is multiplied times itself thirty times over inside the compound interest formula now completely dominates the wealth map. On a direct basis, there are five huge $552,150 inflation gains on the original home equity, totaling about $2,760,000.

The "explosion" in additional dollars that were created when we effectively multiplied the impact of the growth in the national debt by the impact of the growth in population now moves to an entirely different level of magnitude. Every $1 of real market gains on a home now become $13.27 in total new dollars in 30 years, because of the compounding of the dollars needed to buy everything over those years.

This 1227% increase in dollars, when multiplied times the $22,500 real gain on the original home equity, works out to be

$276,075 in additional home equity. When the home is bought with a mortgage, then this is multiplied times five in the eighth level of the multiplication of wealth, and becomes $1,380,375 in additional home equity. That is an additional 31X increase in the starting $45,000 home equity by itself, not from the growth in the national debt, nor from the growth in the population, but from the growth in the national debt occurring at the same time as the growth in the population (along with other factors).

When we add the ten new blocks that are the downstream results of a 50% increase in real market values, they total $1,492,875 - or almost exactly $1.5 million. Another way of phrasing this is that the $22,500 "seed" of real gains on original home equity that are based on population growth and related factors, are now being multiplied by 66.3 to get the total related increase in home equity. The real gains are only 1.5% of the total gains for which they are the root source, and the entire rest of the $1.5 million in new dollars is just the multiplication of that starting seed by the sixth, seventh and eighth levels of the multiplication of wealth when inflation is 9% and compounding.

If we start with a growing population and a shrinking pool of land to be developed where much of the population wants to live, and we multiply that upward pressure on prices times the full power of compound interest on higher rates of inflation due to the out of control national debt, and then we multiply again because we originally paid for most of the property with someone else's money but kept all the population and inflation gains for ourselves, then the combination is truly explosive, multiplying population-related price increases by 66.3X with this round number illustration.

When we add the new $1.5 million in home equity gains that result from a 50% increase in real market values over 30 years, to the $3 million home equity gain from amortization and inflation on the original home price developed in the previous chapter, then the total value of the home that is now owned outright is up to about $4.5 million. That represents an almost exact 100 to 1 increase in home equity, relative to the original $45,000 in equity at the time of purchase.

The destruction of 92.5% of the real value of the current national debt, and 92.5% of the real value of current savings, when flipped and turned into wealth by buying a home with a mortgage, and then further multiplied with a real gain in market value, becomes a 100 to 1 increase in home equity.

The round number outcome of a 100 to 1 increase makes it simple to determine the purchasing power results as well. There are $100 in the future for every dollar today, a dollar in the future will only buy 7.5 cents compared to today, so in inflation-adjusted terms, there was a 7.5 to 1 real increase in homeowner equity. The starting $45,000 in home equity becomes $337,500 in real home equity, when the $4.5 million future home price is multiplied by 7.5%, in order to take into account the 92.5% destruction of the purchasing power of a dollar.

If we go back to our economic theoretician, they might be getting quite agitated, as they make the other $4.2 million in home price disappear, while shouting "Not real! Not real! Just an illusion!" They would be exactly correct if we are just looking at changes in purchasing power in isolation. It is a 7.5X increase in real home equity. And for inflation-adjusted dollars, that is an outstanding result.

That said, when we move to how real people behave and typically live their actual lives in the real world - the full $4.5 million will be there for people who make one decision, it will likely be $0 for many of the people who make the opposite decision, and the gap in financial security is indeed likely to be the greatest ever.

In practice, every dollar of the $4.5 million in future home equity will be there, and every dollar will be of equal importance. The "other" 4.2 million dollars in home equity would not be nothing, they would not be "just" inflation, but rather, they would represent one of the greatest financial success stories of all time. This could be true for tens of millions of homeowners together, just as the natural flow of wealth from having bought a home with a mortgage.

The starting point is what was reviewed in the previous chapter. In practice, the typical person is unlikely to have a plan for investing for inflation (if they think about it at all), half the time they won't start a retirement account, and for the half who do - the degree of savings in practice and the results are not as impressive for the median, the households in the middle, as one might hope for. Some people will do what is needed and do it well, but in practice when it comes to how typical people live their lives, the ones who build the large investment portfolios over the decades are the minority and not the majority.

Decades of higher rates of inflation is a toxic and extremely difficult environment for maintaining the value of what one has, let alone finding a way to increase the inflation-adjusted value of savings. All else being equal, the higher the rate of inflation, the less likely it is that a typical person will be able to keep up with inflation, and the greater the degree of financial damage that results.

When we discount for inflation-adjusted dollars and make most of the future price of a home "disappear", what are we really doing? We are assuming into existence a perfect strategy for investing for inflation and then treating its value as nothing. The natural process of buying a home when homes keep up with inflation is to have a perfectly successful inflation hedge with a major part of one's net worth, that steadily works away in the background, generating new dollars in home equity even as even more dollars are required each year to buy everything else.

The new homeowners may not realize that they are doing this, they may think that they are buying a nice home in a good school district just as a choice for where they want to live their lives, and using a mortgage because that's the only way they can afford it. But yet, as studied in depth in these books, in the very act of doing so they are also making what will likely turn out to be the best investment decision of their lives. Buying the home commits them to setting up and funding their inflation strategy, having their home keep up with inflation is a superb hedge, and turning inflation into wealth turns homeownership into a brilliant inflation-fighting strategy. The higher the rate of inflation, the more valuable this natural byproduct of buying a home with a mortgage becomes.

If we are looking at both higher rates of inflation and real market value gains over time, then in some ways net worth in 30 years is likely to be the least of the problems for many people; the greater problem may be one of just financially surviving those 30 years. The issue with rising real home prices, as seen in places like San Francisco and Seattle in the 2010s, is that rents don't just increase with inflation, they can also increase with the housing market, and at rates well above the rate of inflation.

In a world where a burger and fries goes for over $100, then as developed in the previous chapter, a $1,200 monthly rent payment becomes a $16,000 monthly rent payment, even as the homeowner makes their final mortgage payment, and owns their $3 million home outright.

When we allow for population growth, the potential increasing concentration of a larger population in areas with little undeveloped land, and the increasing regulatory costs of building new homes for the larger population, then the financial chasm between owning and renting can become much wider.

If the rent payment is going up not just with inflation, but also with increases in real market value - then a renter can no longer just have their income keep up with inflation. With a 50% real market value increase and 9% inflation, the rent isn't up to $16,000 in 30 years, but $24,000 per month. If their income can't keep up, the renter may have to repeatedly downgrade where they live over the years, even as they become much more likely to completely deplete their savings.

Meanwhile, the homeowner has two forms of protection with the principal and interest component of their mortgage payments. Their payments do not increase with inflation, and their payments do not increase with higher home values. Now, escrows for property taxes and homeowner insurance are a different matter, but the actual mortgage portion of their payment is fixed, and does not go up.

This double shelter frees up an increasingly large amount of cash flow every month for the homeowner, as their income rises over time with high rates of inflation but their mortgage payment does not.

The natural relationship for higher rates of inflation and rising real home market values is that for each year that is lived, the homeowner does a little better and the mortgage payment gets a little easier to make, while for the renter, the rent payments become more difficult with each passing year, and the gap steadily grows. Until after 30 years, the homeowner is sitting in their $4.5 million home, with no mortgage payment due, while the renter tries to come up with $24,000 for the next month's rent, with no end in sight.

For the real estate investor, this opens up the possibility of having turned a $45,000 initial investment into owning a $4.5 million investment property outright, with no mortgage AND the ability to get $24,000 per month in rental income, after three decades of what could be pain and suffering for the more general investment markets.

The higher the rate of inflation, then the more important and life changing the homeownership decision becomes. Separately, the higher that real market values go, then the more important and life changing the homeownership decision becomes.

If both factors go higher together - whether because of the national debt and population growth or for other reasons altogether - then the importance of the homeownership decision is quite literally multiplied, with a multiplied importance for daily quality of life over the years and with multiplied importance for building financial security over the years.

A Resilient History Of Wealth Creation

So is buying a home a speculation on higher rates of inflation and higher real market values for homes?

Not in the slightest.

There are 19 total chapters in Books 1 & 2, and the first 17 chapters were an intensive study of the past. When looking at the past in detail, whether it was from 1975 to 2019, or 1940 to 2019, the history of homeownership in the United States has been an outstanding success.

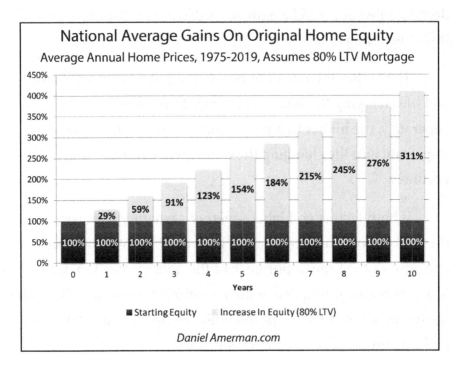

Based on an intensive study of the 395 possible 1-10 year homeownership periods between 1975 and 2019, the national averages for all those millions of homeowners were to see their home equity almost double in three years, to triple home equity in seven years, and to quadruple home equity in ten years (if they purchased their home with a very common 80% LTV mortgage).

Those are amazing results. They are not any form of speculation about what the future holds. They are the lived results of the homeownership experience for Americans across the decades.

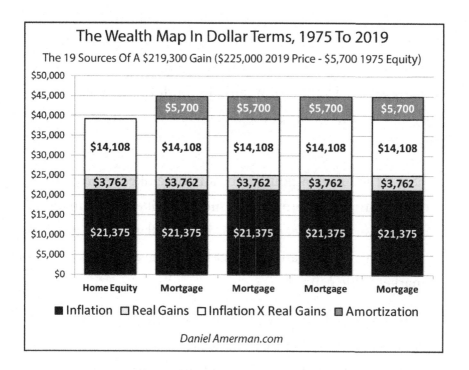

When we look at the past, we can also identify all 19 sources of the long term creation of homeowner wealth over 44 years, put numbers on their individual contributions - and see how they all worked together.

The combined result was another amazing number - a national average almost 40 to1 increase in home equity.

By studying how wealth was actually created in the past, we can get some really good insights into how wealth might potentially be created in the future.

It wasn't real increases in market value on the equity contribution by itself, as that produced only 1.7% of the wealth map. It wasn't just paying off the mortgage either, as that contributed only about 10% of the wealth map.

The rest - which is the overwhelming majority of the wealth map, and the overwhelming source of home equity for older homeowners today - was all in the inflation, the mortgage, and the many multiplications of wealth, for both the original home equity and for the "seed" of the real increase in market value on that equity.

So, if the future is going to be anything like the past, then the odds are that is where the real money is likely to be made over the coming years and decades - it is in the inflation, the mortgage, and the many multiplications, including those associated with any real market value gains.

The six round number illustrations in these last two chapters were not predictions - but were instead explorations of relationships, taking what we learned about what really created the wealth in the past, making a range of assumptions for the future, and then assembling the pieces and seeing how the wealth creation components would work together in each instance.

Even without higher rates of inflation or any increase in real market values - the Homeowner Wealth Formula still works, and the homeowner does really well over time. This is consistent with the history we have explored, where even as the nation went through a long series of unexpected economic and market changes, the natural result of homeownership was nonetheless to still do very well financially over the long term - with no crystal balls needed to predict what will happen, and no surges in inflation or market value needed to deliver the results.

On the other hand, history does include some major surges in inflation and also in real home market values. When those do happen - which historically has been about a quarter of the time as developed in Chapter 8 - then homeowners can indeed "win the lottery", with their home equity increasing by an amount equal to the entire original purchase price of the home in just ten years.

The Homeowner Wealth Formula is a natural flow of wealth that comes with some potentially life changing bonus features that are thrown in as part of the package. If real home prices do soar upwards over the coming decades - the homeowner participates in a multiplied fashion. If the national debt does trigger higher future rates of inflation, then the homeowner is not just protected, but more than protected, in a multiplied fashion.

If both happen together as long term forces over the coming decades, with homes getting ever more expensive in real terms even while the value of the dollar is being shredded, then the eight levels of the multiplication of wealth that are the Homeowner Wealth Formula will all combine again to deliver their maximum wealth creation results for the homeowners of an entire nation.

Other Financial Education Resources

(Available at DanielAmerman.com)

Free Course

Free 20+ chapter online course on the investment implications of cycles of crisis and the containment of crisis for stocks, bonds, real estate and precious metals

Workshops

(check website for more information)

Video Courses

Creating Win-Win-Win Solutions Using Real Estate-Based Asset/Liability Management Strategies

(This is the more sophisticated Turning Inflation Into Wealth course for real estate investors, rather than homeowners.)

Gold Out Of The Box, 2020s Edition

(A different intensive study of 50 years of financial history, this time it is devoted to better understanding secular cycles for gold, and finding superior investment & hedging strategies.)

Investment Strategies For Crisis & The Containment Of Crisis

Author Information

Daniel R. Amerman is a Chartered Financial Analyst and finance MBA with over 30 years of professional financial experience. He is the creator of a number of books and video courses on finance and economics. Articles by Mr. Amerman or referencing his work have appeared in numerous publications and websites, including Reuters, MarketWatch, U.S. News & World Report, MSN Money, Seeking Alpha, Business Insider, ValueWatch, Nasdaq.com, Morningstar.com, TalkMarkets and Financial Sense.

As an investment banking vice president in the 1980s, Mr. Amerman began working with real estate investors and developers in structuring optimum financings for real estate investments. These multimillion dollar deals involved using mortgages and reserves to obtain investment grade ratings on bonds that were issued to fund the acquisition or construction of multifamily residences (apartment buildings), portfolios of multifamily residences, assisted care facilities and nursing homes.

Mr. Amerman also did groundbreaking work as an investment banker and wholesale mortgage banker in the such areas as CMO/REMIC originations as part of portfolio restructurings for financial institutions. This involved working with numerous savings & loan associations in the aftermath of the inflationary crisis of the 1970s and 1980s, and their portfolios of thousands of small and low interest rate mortgages.

It was that combination of working as an expert with sophisticated real estate investment strategies, while also seeing the enormously positive financial impact of what average people were experiencing in small towns and cities all across the nation as the more or less accidental result of having bought homes with mortgages during a time of turmoil and inflation, that would eventually lead to The Homeowner Wealth Formula book and series.

In the 1990s, Mr. Amerman worked as an independent quantitative analyst, providing expert structural, analytical and mathematical verification services for the trust departments of major banks, investment banks, and rating agencies, mostly in real estate and mortgage related areas. During those same years Mr. Amerman wrote his first two books on investment and security analysis for institutional investors, that were published by McGraw-Hill (and subsidiary): *Mortgage Securities*, and *Collateralized Mortgage Obligations: Unlock The Secrets Of Mortgage Derivatives*.

Many of the highly sophisticated strategies used by institutional investors, major banks and hedge funds for real estate and mortgage investment were almost completely unknown by average individual investors, they were of a fundamentally different nature than the usual personal finance and investment strategies. Mr. Amerman decided to focus on developing and teaching simpler and understandable strategies for individuals, that were also of a fundamentally different nature than the usual consumer financial education. This led to the original Turning Inflation Into Wealth online course, workshops and DVD video course by 2008. (As a mortgage derivatives expert, Mr. Amerman also wrote extensively in 2007 and 2008 about the dangers posed by mortgage derivatives in a time of greed when Wall Street was taking enormous risks, and how that could bring down the financial system in a flash.)

In the years that followed, the workshops in particular provided a double-sided education. Mr. Amerman taught non-traditional investment strategies to audiences of motivated investors, and he in turn learned how to best communicate with audiences that often consisted mostly of self-made millionaires who had made their money in a wide variety of fields. Instead of the dry world of institutional finance and investment analysis books - how to get a highly successful professional or entrepreneur to sit up on the edge of their seat, as he or she put together the pieces for a different approach and new strategies for preserving and expanding the wealth they had built?

The way that the information was presented in the workshops and video courses was refined over the years, even as the extensive data bases and analyses underlying the real estate and gold investment courses were expanded and improved. The end result is the unique information and presentation in The

Homeowner Wealth Formula book and series, as well as the extensive underlying research.

Much more information on other research, analyses, books, video courses and workshops is available at:

DanielAmerman.com.

Sources & Methodology Notes

The source for inflation information is the Consumer Price Index for Urban Consumers (CPI-U), as provided by the U.S. Bureau of Labor Statistics (BLS).

The historical 30 year mortgage rates are from the Federal Home Loan Mortgage Corporation, which is better known as Freddie Mac.

Obtaining timely and consistent national real estate statistics can be challenging relative to collecting information on securities such as stocks and bonds, for there is no daily closing price, and price change reporting may be delayed by months as the data is gathered. There are also the issues that where people live changes just a bit each year, as does the year of construction, size and amenities of an average home.

The standard is therefore to use a "pairs-based" methodology, where sales of the same home in different years are used to track real estate price changes, rather than changes in mean or median home prices. This does limit the historical database, with the Freddie Mac House Price Index used in this book going back only to 1975.

The "pairs-based" Case-Schiller index is the norm for media reporting of national housing price movements, however, the most commonly reported measure focuses only on the 20 large metropolitan areas, and these can exhibit very different price behavior than the rest of the country.

The Freddie Mac House Price Index used herein includes all 50 states, as well as the other 300+ metro areas, making it a much better national measure, and it is also based on a pairs methodology which accounts for changes in average home size and amenities over the years. But the national average index slightly changes each year, in a way that is retroactive for all the previous years on the basis of "geographic weighting", which likely primarily reflects estimated population shifts, although Freddie Mac won't release the methodology or the weights.

The data base and analyses used herein were developed over a number of years, and the decision was made to not completely change all prior analyses each time that Freddie Mac decided to retroactively change their index. The index numbers were all accurate at the time that they were downloaded, and they are updated regularly. The earlier years of the index were slightly different for previous years than what Freddie Mac was reporting in 2020, which is likely to be slightly different from the index in 2021, and is likely to be different again in 2022, due to this ongoing retroactive revision of their data base.

The consumer financial information and median home value for 2019 are from the Federal Reserve's 2019 Survey Of Consumer Finances, and do not use a "pairs-based" methodology.

The once per decade median home values from 1940 through 2000 used in Chapter 5 are from the U.S. Census Bureau and do not use a "pairs-based" methodology.

Made in the USA
Las Vegas, NV
03 February 2024

85243212R00134